side by side

by

8 Conversations to Build Your Confidence in Christ

JAYME HULL

WESTBOW
PRESS®
A DIVISION OF THOMAS NELSON
& ZONDERVAN

Interior Image Credit: Kristen Ingrebretson

Scripture quotations marked (NIV) are taken from the Holy Bible, New International Version®, NIV®. Copyright © 1973, 1978, 1984, 2011 by Biblica, Inc.™ Used by permission of Zondervan. All rights reserved worldwide. www.zondervan.com The "NIV" and "New International Version" are trademarks registered in the United States Patent and Trademark Office by Biblica, Inc.™

Scripture quotations are from the ESV® Bible (The Holy Bible, English Standard Version®), copyright © 2001 by Crossway, a publishing ministry of Good News Publishers. Used by permission. All rights reserved.

Scripture quotations marked (NLT) are taken from the Holy Bible, New Living Translation, copyright ©1996, 2004, 2015 by Tyndale House Foundation. Used by permission of Tyndale House Publishers, Inc., Carol Stream, Illinois 60188. All rights reserved.

Scripture quotations marked MSG are taken from THE MESSAGE, copyright © 1993, 1994, 1995, 1996, 2000, 2001, 2002 by Eugene H. Peterson. Used by permission of NavPress. All rights reserved. Represented by Tyndale House Publishers, Inc.

Scripture quotations taken from the New American Standard Bible® (NASB), Copyright © 1960, 1962, 1963, 1968, 1971, 1972, 1973, 1975, 1977, 1995 by The Lockman Foundation Used by permission. www.Lockman.org

The New Testament in Modern English by J.B Phillips copyright © 1960, 1972 J. B. Phillips. Administered by The Archbishops' Council of the Church of England. Used by Permission.

WestBow Press books may be ordered through booksellers or by contacting:

WestBow Press
A Division of Thomas Nelson & Zondervan
1663 Liberty Drive
Bloomington, IN 47403
www.westbowpress.com
1 (866) 928-1240

ISBN: 978-1-9736-4579-5 (sc)
ISBN: 978-1-9736-4581-8 (hc)
ISBN: 978-1-9736-4580-1 (e)

Library of Congress Control Number: 2018913876

Print information available on the last page.

WestBow Press rev. date: 12/10/2018

As Paul says in 2 Thessalonians 2:16-17 (NIV)
"May our Lord Jesus Christ himself and God our Father,
who loved us and by his grace gave us
eternal encouragement and good hope, encourage
your hearts and strengthen you in every good deed and word."

This one's for You, Lord!
I'm forever grateful for
Your eternal encouragement!

CONTENTS

FOREWORD

God loves us too much to leave us where we are. He always has more for us to become and experience than we could ever imagine (Eph. 3:20). Yet, even though we may want to become a better person, we often don't see ourselves clearly. We tend to assume things are not as bad as they really are or that our situation is impossible or too difficult to change. We might talk about change, but, at the end of the day, we too often remain the same.

Fortunately, God has innumerable means at His disposal to initiate transformation. God is an expert at changing people for the better. Two of God's most effective tools are people and questions. Some of the most powerful words God says to us will come from someone else's mouth. Whenever we encounter Christians, we also encounter the Holy Spirit who indwells them. Never underestimate what God can say through a fellow believer. People view us more objectively than we see ourselves. King Solomon said, "The mouth of the righteous is a fountain of life" (Prov. 10:11); "Wisdom is found on the lips of the discerning" (Prov. 10:13); "The tongue of the righteous is pure silver" (Prov. 20); "The lips of the righteous feed many" (Prov. 10:21). Those who desire to grow will surround themselves with wise people who can speak truth into their life.

A second way God initiates change is through questions. God has been asking people questions since the Garden of Eden. "Where are you?" (Gen. 3:9). "Where is your brother Abel?" (Gen. 4:9). "What is that in your hand?" (Ex. 4:2). "Who do you say that I am?" (Matt. 16:15). "Simon, son of John, do you love me more than these?" (John 21:15). God's questions lay us bare before Him. We should not be surprised when God uses questions from godly friends to challenge and grow us.

For this reason, I am delighted my friend Jayme Hull has written *Side By Side*. She is uniquely gifted at walking alongside people and asking them thought-provoking, life-changing questions in a delightful, disarming way. Her writing is upbeat, biblically centered, to the point, and extremely practical. She goes straight to the heart of the matter, offering hope rather than heaping on guilt. She takes an interesting look at Scripture and brings the reader face-to-face with divine truths.

This is a great book to study with others. It is filled with truths that will spark meaningful discussions. It is the kind of book people will want to return to often to find additional nuggets of gold still lying near the surface. I heartily recommend it to anyone who enjoys growing in the company of friends.

Dr. Richard Blackaby
President of Blackaby Ministries International and
co-author of *Experiencing God, and Spiritual Leadership Coaching*

ARE YOU READY TO CONNECT?

Does life feel like something is missing spiritually? Are you tired of doing life alone? If so, this study is for you.

I hear from women and men all over the country who feel the same way you do. They are saying, "I'm dry." "I'm tired." "I long for real connections with people face to face." The same thoughts and phrases enter into my conversations with the people I mentor, the discussions I have with those I guide as a spiritual leadership coach, or when I speak to groups. So what's the solution?

As you connect with God more intimately, you'll be able to form more meaningful connections with others. So, join me on a journey to build your confidence in Christ. Yes! There is hope! This study is about the power of stories to ignite your passion, once again, for your Lord and Savior and His Word.

Before you begin this Bible Study, I want to share with you the verse on my heart as I wrote this study. Philippians 1:27 (ESV) says, "that I may hear of you that you are standing firm in one spirit, with one mind striving side by side for the faith of the gospel."

Mentoring is my passion, and sharing the good news of the Gospel of Jesus Christ is my purpose. I love to encourage and equip others to dig into God's Word and to become a part of a mentoring relationship.

Faith is a journey that we dare not take alone. We need courage to ask difficult questions. We need wisdom to discern God's leading. While Jesus is always present with us, a safe person—a mentor, or a small group setting—can help us connect and find God in the messiness of our questions, doubts, and confusion.

Together, we'll begin to seek out safe people who can walk with us amid our daily questions. Along the journey, you can rest and know that

God is the great orchestrator of all good gifts, including, the gift of a mentor or a small group.

I invite you to step out, challenge yourself. As you do, hold loosely to your dreams and tightly to your heavenly Father. Be brave. Be yourself. Growing in your faith isn't easy, but I promise you, the journey is well worth every step. And know this - you never have to walk alone. Come along with me. Now is the time to do life, *side by side*!

Let's get started,
Jayme

Does God Care About My Story?

*Then those who feared the Lord spoke with each other, and the Lord **listened** to what they said. In his presence, a scroll of remembrance was written to record the names of those who feared him and always thought about the honor of his name. "They will be my people," says the Lord of Heaven's Armies. "On the day when I act in judgment, they will be my own special treasure. I will spare them as a father spares an obedient child. Malachi 3:16-17 (NLT)*

Day 1: Can God Really Hear Me?

All I ever do is listen to other people. Can you relate? As if your actual job description is "sounding board for other peoples' problems"? You listen to your family chat away, or you hear about the drama at work for hours at a time. But what about you?

You have thoughts and stories to share, but it doesn't feel like anyone is listening. Not even God.

People ask me if mentoring really matters. They don't see how talking about life with a mentor can make a difference, but in Malachi 3:16-17, we find God enjoys listening in on our conversations. He cares about what you care about. When you sit down with a brother or sister in Christ to talk about Him, He does more than listen. He writes it down.

God takes notes on your conversations.

Take a moment for that to sink in. We're not talking about an award-winning actor or a *New York Times* bestselling author or the leader of a Fortune 500 company. We're talking about God, who spoke the sun into the sky, who wove your DNA together, who keeps the universe spinning. He knows your thoughts, your dreams, your future. He can do anything—literally. When you open yourself to another person (especially your mentor) about your faith, share your heart, encourage someone else, confess your weaknesses, or pray with another believer, God pays attention. To you.

How does this make you feel?

_____

What's the first thing you would tell God if you knew for sure He was listening?

_____

> Malachi was a prophet, God's representative on Earth, around 430 B.C., and he wrote the last book of the Old Testament. While the book of Malachi only has four chapters, it's pivotal, because afterward God stopped speaking to His creation through prophets. He didn't speak to us again for 400 years. So when you read Malachi, remember it's God's last words for His people before Jesus was born.

Let's check out Malachi 3:16 together.
What are the people in Malachi 3:16 doing?

_____

What does Malachi 3:16 say God does when His people talk about Him?

_____

What does God have written down and why?

_____

When you make a point to have intentional conversations with others, purposefully honoring God's name, directing others to His Word, sharing about His power and character, He listens. He hears.

Depending on what version of Scripture you're reading, Malachi 3:16 may use the term "book of remembrance." So let's take a quick trip over to the Book of Esther where another book of remembrance is mentioned.

Read Esther 2:23. What is the name of the book where the events were recorded?

_____

In whose presence was the event recorded?

_____

Read Esther 6:1. What did the king want to read?

_____

Thinking about both of these examples, how important was it for the information in the "book of remembrance" to be accurate?
Why?

_____

Let's dig into the following verses. How does each verse relate to how God pays attention to our conversations?
Psalm 33:18

_____

Psalm 34:15

_____

Proverbs 15:29

_____

According to the following verses, what questions can you ask God?
John 15:7

_____

James 1:5

_____

> Malachi 3:16 is all about mentoring. It's God's take on what happens when you share your story with another person or when you acknowledge Him as part of your life. When you honor Him, you make Him happy. God loves conversation.

Read Hebrews 10:24-25 and describe the three "let us" statements:

1. _____

2. _____

3. _____

Look at Hebrews 10:24 again. What specific ways can you encourage another believer toward love and good deeds?

_____

_____

Recall a time when your mentor or a special person in your life spurred you on.

_____

_____

Read 1 Thessalonians 5:11.
Who has been an encourager in your life?

_____

_____

What impact did it make in your life?

_____

_____

Select your favorite verse from Day 1 then flip forward to Day 5 of this chapter and record it in the top box. For the rest of today spend time in prayer meditating and living out the verse you selected.

A Prayer

Heavenly Father, You're amazing. Thanks for being my Creator God. How humbling to know You created the universe and put the stars in place, and still You desire to live in my heart and listen to my conversations.

Somewhere along the line, I stopped believing You were listening to me. Forgive me. I'm excited to start our relationship side by side on a fresh new path. Anoint me with Your Holy Spirit and help me become the godly person You created me to be. I know it will be hard but go ahead and change me. Mold me into a new creation with passion and joy. Help me to grow in my faith and my relationship with You. Amen.

Day 2: Walking Along the Road

Chaos and noise walk hand-in-hand in the twenty-first century. Can I get an amen? Sometimes you have to intentionally create quiet so you can hear yourself think.

I walk my dog, Rascal. When I'm out stretching my legs and focusing on the quiet, I spend time in prayer. I like to use this time to think and dream with God.

Many times I want Jesus to come to earth to walk alongside me or sit with me for an hour to have a cup of coffee and discuss my urgent issue. I know He is always with me, but there are times when I need Him to appear like Jesus, with skin on. How about you?

Where do you go to have one-on-one conversations with God?

What do you talk about?

Jesus loves conversations so much He disguised Himself so He could get in on one and reveal truth to the believers. This story takes place the night after Jesus' resurrection from the dead.

> The four Gospels (Matthew, Mark, Luke, and John) mark the first Word from God to Israel in 400 years. And what was God talking about? His Son: Jesus.

Read the story in Luke 24:13-35 and answer the following questions: What were the two men talking about?

_____

What kept the two men from recognizing Jesus?

_____

Notice here, Jesus comes alongside these two followers and shows no condemnation for their doubts, disappointments, and unbelief. Instead He offers healing answers and hope.

What did the two men tell Jesus about what had happened in Jerusalem?

_____

How did Jesus respond?

_____

What distractions in your life cause you to miss Jesus?

_____

How do you think the two men felt after Jesus disappeared?

_____

God is all about relationships. In the Old Testament, God made a point of building relationships with His followers through signs, prophets, miracles, and personal visits. **He hasn't changed.** Relationships still come first with God, and He wants you to have a relationship with Him. He also wants you to have mentoring relationships with other believers too.

Let's read Matthew 18:19-20 and realize the power in His name and strength we receive when we gather together.

There is power in the name of God. Kay Arthur wrote a study called *Lord, I Want to Know You* that has taught people the power of God's name.

> **"God's name represents His character, His attributes, His nature. To know His name is to know Him."**
> **– Kay Arthur**

Know God Better—Through His Awesome Names

When we study the names of God we get a glimpse of God's wonderful character. Psalm 9:10 encourages us, "And those who know your name put their trust in you, for you, O Lord, have not forsaken those who seek you." **Instructions:** Look up the verse in the right-hand column and match it to the letter beside the Name of God in the left-hand column.

Names of God	Bible Verse
A. Jehovah-Shalom, The Lord of Peace	_____ Exodus 15:26
B. El Roi, The God Who Sees	_____ John 6:35
C. Jehovah-Jireh, The Lord Will Provide	_____ 1 John 2:1
D. Jehovah-Rapha, The Lord Who Heals	_____ Revelation 19:11
E. Jehovah-Shammah, The Lord Is There	_____ Genesis 22:14
F. Advocate	_____ Judges 6:24
G. Bread of Life	_____ Ezekiel 48:35
H. Faithful and True	_____ Genesis 16:13

There is so much power in the name of God. Which of the names of God listed above is your favorite at this moment in life and why?

_____

> Take a moment and say a prayer to God right now. Call Him by one of His names and thank Him for always listening to you.

God isn't just about relationships. He's about remembering. He has promised over and over again in Scripture to never abandon His children, to never forget them, to always provide.

How do the following verses demonstrate how important remembrance is to God?
Luke 12:6-7

_____

Isaiah 49:15-16

_____

We know God hears our conversations, and we know when we are open and honest with each other and acknowledge His work in our lives, He is pleased. Imagine what it would be like for God to like your Tweet or share your Instagram post.

Look up Malachi 3:17 and **write down what God does** for those who honor Him:

1. _____

2. _____

Those people who He writes about, the ones who honor Him and acknowledge Him, He calls them His special treasures. Remember today, you are a jewel to the Lord, and He treasures you, values you, cherishes you as someone eternally precious to Him.

Select your favorite verse from Day 2 then flip forward to Day 5 of this chapter and record it in the top box. For the rest of today spend time in prayer meditating and living out the verse you selected.

A Prayer

Dear Lord Jesus, my Jehovah-Shammah, The Lord Who Is There, teach me how to know You more. I need You to come alongside me and teach Your Word to me like You did with the men on the road to Emmaus. There's so much I don't know or understand, but I'm willing to learn. I want to hear Your voice. Please Lord. Will You walk with me too? I need new ears to hear and I'm willing to go the extra mile. Speak Lord. I need You to guide me through each day, Amen.

Day 3: Your Choices Matter

Catherine Marshall: Obstacle or Opportunity

Born at the beginning of the 20th Century, Catherine Marshall contracted tuberculosis as a young woman, which left her an invalid for several years.[1] Even though she recovered, she was never quite the same physically.

Her husband, Peter, pastored the New York Avenue Presbyterian Church in Washington, D.C. and was appointed twice as the Chaplain of the United States Senate. He died unexpectedly at 46 years of age.[2] Catherine became the sole provider for herself and her nine-year-old son at a time in history when being a single mother was unusual. She needed financial help, or she and her son might starve.

Catherine prayed for help, but the answer she got wasn't what she expected. Since childhood, Catherine dreamed of being a writer, and she'd kept a journal. God's answer directed her to write and trust her financial security to Him, no matter how risky it might seem.

This was the time God had chosen to fulfill her childhood dream.

In Psalm 139:16, God tells us He has a plan and a dream for every person's life before they are even born.

What was your dream as a little kid?

_____

Did you ever tell anyone about your dream or write it in a diary or journal?

_____

God asked Catherine to share her story with others by using her childhood dream to become a writer. Would you ever consider sharing a God-story from your life to help someone?

Circle One: Yes   Possibly   Doubtful   No

Do you have a dream right now? Are you talking to God about your dream? Are you willing to pursue your dream?

Is there anything holding you back from sharing and being authentic with others about your walk with the Lord?

_____

This wasn't a choice Catherine expected she'd have to make, but life is full of those kinds of moments. She had a choice. She could do what made sense and sell all her belongings and give up her life to make ends meet, or she could do what God was moving her to do—to write a story. Would she stop her dream in its tracks and run from the obstacles she faced? Would she surrender to fear and uncertainty?

Can you guess which one she chose?

In 1951, Catherine Marshall published *A Man Called Peter*, a biography of her late husband. The book became an overnight success and was even developed into a film, which was released in 1955. Catherine kept writing and editing, and in her lifetime she produced more than 30 books, which have sold more than 16 million copies. Maybe you've read the book or watched the TV series *Christy*, based on her mother's life in the Appalachian Mountains, or *Julie*, based on her life growing up in Depression-era West Virginia.

Marshall risked stepping out to do what God said—to tell her story, but to her, it wasn't a risk because it was God who asked. She decided to trust God. It was her choice, and she saw her dream fulfilled.

> **"The search for God begins at the point of need." - Catherine Marshall**

What will it take to make the choice today to totally trust God with your struggles?

_____

What instructions do we find about prayer and trust from the following verses?
Jeremiah 17:7-8

_____

Philippians 4:6

_____

The Widow of Zarephath: Choosing God in Spite of Circumstances

> The Old Testament book of 1 Kings is one of the history books of the Bible, and much of it tells the story of the prophet Elijah. Remember how Malachi was a prophet? Elijah was similar, except he lived much earlier in history. When we pick up his story in chapter 17, he's on the run from an evil king, and God directs him to a city called Zarephath where he will meet an unnamed widow.

Open your Bible and read 1 Kings 17:8-16. In this story, we meet a widow who also came face-to-face with an unexpected choice between life and death.

Stop for a second. Did you notice? **The widow doesn't have a name.** Kind of stinks, doesn't it? But maybe you understand.

Do you ever feel like the widow and the rest of the unnamed and ignored? Invisible?

I know I have people calling me "John's wife" or "Jered's mom" all the time, but let's go back to 1 Kings 17:9-10. Don't miss this critical part of the story. God says: "Go at once to Zarephath … I have directed a widow there—" STOP.

What did you just read?

God Himself directed the widow. He had a very specific plan for her life, and it was to serve the great prophet, Elijah, and receive a miraculous blessing. Verse 10 tells us: "So he went to Zarephath, and when Elijah came to the town gate, and she was there…."

God's divine appointment. God's perfect timing. God's perfect plan for your life.

Do you believe God knows your name? Circle One:

Absolutely   Unsure   Doubtful   Not Really

In our story, the widow lives in Zarephath. Zarephath, which is believed to be in modern-day Lebanon[3], was an ancient city on the road along the seashore of the Mediterranean. Picture the scene. It's a warm, muggy day on the shoreline of the Mediterranean Ocean. The air smells like olives and dust. And a starving widow is out collecting sticks so she can heat her oven to make a last meal for herself and her son.

Then along comes Elijah the prophet, hot, tired, and dirty from his travels. Elijah asks her for a cup of water and something to eat, and the widow responds honestly: "I don't have a single piece of bread in the house. And I have only a handful of flour left in the jar and a little cooking oil in the bottom of the jug. I was just gathering a few sticks to cook this last meal, and then my son and I will die." (1 Kings 17:12, NLT)

Put yourself in the widow's shoes. How would you respond to Elijah? Choose One:

☐ "Clueless man! He only thinks about his needs."
☐ "I'm at the end of my rope. I have no choice but to trust him."
☐ "Why do I always get into these messes? I might as well do what he says."

Imagine your mentor or someone you deeply respect showed up on your doorstep unexpectedly, asking for something to eat when they knew you didn't have enough for yourself or your family.

What would you tell them?

_____

This woman had lost her husband, and she and her son had only enough to make one last meal before they would starve to death. Then, Elijah the prophet requests she share their last bite of food with him, but he offers her a promise from God (1 Kings 17:14). The widow had a decision to make. She could either tell Elijah to buzz off, or she could do as he asked.

Talk about a risk. The widow had every right to turn him down. It was, after all, her last meal. He had no right to demand anything from her. But instead of seeing his request as a risk, the widow saw who Elijah was. More importantly, she saw who he worked for. And instead of judging the risk by what was at stake for her and her son, she decided to trust Elijah and Elijah's God. Notice how God, El Roi, The God Who Sees, saw her need and intervened in her life.

Put yourself in the widow's shoes as she walks home to bake her last cake of bread. She emptied the last bit of flour and the last drops of olive oil, and she gave part of it to Elijah. Her son must have been horrified. Here was his mother giving away the last bit of food they had to a stranger. Her son had to know what it meant for him and his mother.

Are you a people pleaser? Do you struggle with what your teenager or family will think of you when you make a tough decision?
Circle One: Absolutely   Always   Sometimes   Never

Be encouraged! If you are struggling with tough choices and stress from your job, you don't have to do life alone. Invite God to come alongside you. When God shows up, lives are changed. If you know the story, or if you read ahead, you know what happened next. What Elijah had promised her came true (1 Kings 17:15-16). She and her family received a miracle, and there was always enough flour and olive oil for them.

Share your story. Where have you seen God reveal Himself?

_____

_____

_____

What prayer need are you still waiting on for an answer?

_____

_____

_____

On a scale of 1 to 10 (one being empty and 10 being overflowing with blessings), where is your oil supply right now? _____
(Date: _____)

Color in the chart to represent your oil supply level.

1   2   3   4   5   6   7   8   9   10

"Never be afraid to trust an unknown future to a known God." – Corrie Ten Boom

Sometimes what God asks us to do doesn't seem logical. Sometimes what He asks us to do is impossible. Whatever He's asking you to do is risky, but are you judging the risk by what you'll lose or by who He is? Are you willing to take a risk and trust God with your story?

You can trust God with your future. You can give Him a blank canvas, and He'll make it into a masterpiece. But you have to hand it over first.

What action are you willing to take this week to show God you completely trust Him with your future?

Select your favorite verse from Day 3 then flip forward to Day 5 of this chapter and record it in the top box. For the rest of today spend time in prayer meditating and living out the verse you selected.

A Prayer

Holy Spirit, You are my Advocate and Counselor. I give You complete permission to move in my life right now. I can't do life alone. I need You by my side. Fill me with a fresh faith to live more intentionally. I'm fighting fears. My heart is anxious. I long to live with Your peace inside of me on a daily basis. I need You right now in my life and invite You to draw me under Your wings of love and protection, Amen.

Day 4: Your Story Matters to God

Remember elementary school? You'd slog through a day of reading, writing, and 'rithmatic, but somewhere in there, the teacher would announce: "It's story time." Eagerly, you'd grab carpet squares with your classmates and find a spot on the floor to listen. Maybe you sat at your desk. Then, the teacher or the guest would start reading. Some added accents and funny voices, and you'd laugh along with them.

For me, story time at school was the highlight of my day, and in some ways, it still is.

Everybody has a story. We all start somewhere, and we're all on a journey of becoming something different from when we started. Sharing our story with those around us can be scary at first, but nobody else has lived our lives. How can someone else experience it unless you tell it?

God made you exactly the way you are. He gave you your quirks and eccentricities. He designed your beautiful mind, heart, and soul, and no one else can duplicate you. You are unique and special in every way possible, from the tips of your toes to the top of your head, regardless of where you come from, where you're going, or how you get there. No one else has lived your story.

What's your story? Where does God fit in? Because He does, and He has a plan for you.

> *Before you start writing your story, ask God to help you. Remember, your story is a small part of His story.*

Write Your Story

What was life like before you gave God complete control?

_____

_____

_____

How were you exposed to the gospel of Jesus Christ?

_____

_____

_____

How did your life change as you started your career or family?

_____

_____

_____

> Instead, you must worship Christ as Lord of your life. And if someone asks about your hope as a believer, always be ready to explain it. But do this in a gentle and respectful way. Keep your conscience clear. Then if people speak against you, they will be ashamed when they see what a good life you live because you belong to Christ.
> 1 Peter 3:15-16

Looking in the Mirror Face to Face

Identify three factors hindering you from sharing your God-story.

1. _____
2. _____
3. _____

Can you control any of the factors you listed?

_____

How can God and your mentor help you conquer what's holding you back in your faith?

_____

_____

Your story doesn't have to be impressive. It has to be real. And you have to be willing to share it, otherwise you'll never connect with another person on a deep, meaningful level. True relationships begin when we drop our walls and embrace authenticity with each other.

God is the author of your story, regardless if you climb mountains or jump out of airplanes or work a desk job or travel with the military or homeschool your children, and He has a purpose for you. **It's your job to tell your story, and God will do the rest.**

Let's Ask the Tough Questions

At this time, what is the greatest satisfaction in your life?

_____

What is the best way your mentor can encourage and help you?

_____

What do you hope to get from reading and completing this Bible study?

_____

Everyone needs to continue to grow in their faith. Where do you need to grow in your relationship with God?

_____

Are you willing to dig deep and be teachable about yourself and God's call on your life?

Circle One: Wholeheartedly   Not Sure   Hesitantly   Not Yet

The next step in this process is to **begin praying**. Ask God for help as you begin your journey to a deeper relationship with God. Ask Him to stretch and enrich your mentoring relationship.

Then, when you've completed this study, come back to this page. See if your answers are the same. See what God has done for you.

> **"The underlying principle of prayer, which overwhelmed me, is that God desires to be intimate with me, and He wants this relationship so much that He invites, encourages, and helps me pray."**
> **Cynthia Heald,** *Becoming a Woman of Prayer*

Worth the Risk, Worth the Reward

Whether you're telling your story to a stranger or risking your well-being on God's promises, following Jesus always requires some risk. Risk is a part of life. You take a risk every time you step out of your home, every time you drive your car, and every time you try something new. It's true, some risks are bigger and scarier than others.

God's Word instructs us to share our story. Read the following verses:

- Psalm 96:2-4
- Joel 1:3

Risk is woven into the tapestry of our lives. Uncertainty lurks in every tomorrow. Living is risky. But we shouldn't judge risk by what's at stake. Instead, we should judge risk by what—or Who—we're trusting to uphold us.

In Esther 4:13-14, we see how Mordecai took the risk to challenge Esther to a greater purpose for her life, and likewise we see how Esther took a the life-or-death risk to follow God's calling: "Then I will go to the King, though it's against the laws: and if I perish, I perish."

Be encouraged. You and I can take a risk too.

What has been your biggest risk and challenge you have had to face in your faith?

_____

_____

If you've never taken a risk, what has been holding you back? What are you willing to do to resolve the tug of war in your heart?

_____

_____

You don't have to do life alone, my friend. We've learned, starting in Malachi 3:16, God cares about your conversations so much He takes notes. Verse 17 tells us He sees you as His most precious jewel, and He values you more than you can imagine.

God treasures you, so let yourself be cherished. It's difficult sometimes, but let your mind accept how much He loves you. God has great plans for you, and even though what He asks or says is unexpected, He's big enough to work everything out.

> You are a beautiful book in God's amazing library of grace, and your story has a good ending.

Consider these four actions when making decisions or taking risks:

1. **Seek Wise Counsel:** Meet with a trusted mentor.
2. **Read Scripture:** Make a solid decision based on Scripture and not fear.
3. **Pursue Peace:** Evaluate your motives and search your heart for hidden motives.
4. **Listen to the Holy Spirit through Prayer:** Ask the Holy Spirit to give you a fresh faith when making decisions or taking risks.

Select your favorite verse from Day 4 then flip forward to Day 5 of this chapter and record it in the top box. For the rest of today spend time in prayer meditating and living out the verse you selected.

A Prayer

Dear God, El Roi, the God who sees me, reveal Yourself to me today. I'm desperate for Your love. I admit I can't do life alone. Do whatever it takes to help me grow in my walk with You. I long to be consistent in reading Your Word and spending time in prayer. I've always struggled to be consistent in my faith, but I want to change. Help me change. Don't leave me. Stay by my side. I need You, Jesus. Please Lord, go ahead and write my story and show me what Your plan is for my life and my family. Help me be humble and brave enough to take a risk and step out. I'm deciding to follow Your lead instead of going my way. I know You are my true Protector and Provider. In the powerful name of Jesus I pray, Amen.

Day 5: A Time To Remember

As you complete each daily section of this study, write down your favorite verse from each day.

Day 1: _____
Day 2: _____
Day 3: _____
Day 4: _____

Journaling the Journey

1. Write what brought you to realize you needed a Savior.

_____

_____

_____

2. Choose one of the names of God from Day 2 and write about what it means to you. How does it affect your life? What would your life look like if you truly believed in God's powerful name?

_____

_____

_____

3. Select a question you would ask Jesus if you could meet Him for coffee. Why is this question important to you? Why haven't you asked Jesus in prayer already?

_____

_____

_____

So shall my word be that goes out from my mouth; it shall not return to me empty, but it shall accomplish that which I purpose, and shall succeed in the thing for which I sent it. Isaiah 55:11 (ESV)

A Prayer

Sovereign Lord, You are my Jehovah-Jireh, my Provider. I'm surrendering my fears and holding onto Your eternal love. No matter how hard I try to meet with You every day and pray, I still fall short. Thank You for Your grace and mercy. Thank You, Lord, for Your forgiveness and faithfulness. Help me with my doubt and discouragement. Your Word says what is impossible with men is possible with God. I'm weak, but today I choose to accept Your divine plan for my life. Help me to grow and have the courage to tell my story to my family and to others. When it runs out, be my strength. Stay by my side, and we will make a great team. In Your Holy Name I pray, Amen.

> **Mentoring Tip: A Mentor leads the way to a smoother path with God's Word as your guide.**

CONVERSATION 2

Can God Help Me Get Past My Guilt?

Then David left his baggage in the care of the baggage keeper, and ran to the battle line and entered in order to greet his brothers. 1 Samuel 17:22 [NASB]

Day 1: Check the Baggage

Getting across an airport terminal is difficult enough without dragging a broken suitcase behind you, right? Have you ever had ten minutes to make your flight and discovered your bag has a bad wheel? It's like a boat trying make headway through the waves with the anchor still down.

And it's not like you have time to stop and fix it. You can't even ask for help. So you press forward, arm straining, back aching, and a broken wheel scraping a dull, tuneless melody on the tiles of the concourse.

How appropriate to find this verse about baggage, right? David, arguably the greatest king of Israel, had a lot to carry.

Most of us think of David as king and forget where he started. We first meet David in the Old Testament book of 1 Samuel 16. He's the youngest of eight sons, a shepherd. And while the Bible tells us he was handsome and brave, within his family he was considered the least important.

So when Samuel appeared and anointed David to be the next king of Israel instead of the seven older brothers, you can imagine there were some hard feelings.

Read 1 Samuel 16:7 and write down why God chose David to be king instead of his brothers.

_____

Why do you think Samuel anointed David in front of his brothers?

_____

If you had been one of the brothers, how would you have felt? Circle as many as apply:

Jealous	Discouraged	Proud	Shocked	Guilt
Hurt	Defeated	Excited	Angry	Other

In your current relationship with God, do you feel passed over or chosen?

_____

What makes you feel that way?

_____

Read 1 Samuel 17:17-22. What was literally in David's baggage?

_____

Who was he delivering the package to?

_____

What did his father ask for?

_____

When Jesse, David's father, sent him to the front lines of the battle, it says something about David as a person. Even as a teenager, a responsibility like this meant David was reliable and trustworthy.

But think about where David came from, and think about what had happened to him. He'd been anointed as the next king in front of his older brothers.

What kind of emotional baggage do you think David was carrying around?

_____

_____

Everybody has baggage. And I'm not talking about the kind you have to check on a flight. I mean the emotional kind, either baggage someone else gave you or baggage you chose to carry. Some of us carry our baggage in small, manageable backpacks. Others of us are crushed beneath the weight of something so huge we can't ever hope to lift it alone.

We all miss the most powerful truth about the baggage in our lives: We don't have to carry it. There's somewhere you can put it.

Add labels to this suitcase. Choose from words below or add your own.

Fragile	Handle with Care	Lost	Rejected
Breakable	Special Cargo	Wrong Destination	Unclaimed

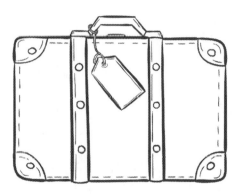

Our parents, our siblings, our peers, our spouses, even our children, nieces, and nephews—whether they say it out loud or not, they all have expectations, and it's impossible to please them all. We try to keep up with culture. We try to keep up with school. We try to keep up with domestic life. We try to keep up with social events and maybe even our church friends. We try and try and try, and we can't do everything we're expected to do.

So feeling guilty is natural, even to be expected. Right?

> Stop what you're doing. Pray right now for God to silence the negative thoughts circling your mind and help you see how much He loves you.

"Today, let's set our minds and hearts on feeling more thankful for what we are than guilty for what we're not. Let's cut the threads of guilt with grace."
– Lysa TerKeurst

What feelings of guilt are tugging on your heart right now?

_____

Where did those feelings come from?

_____

Read Hebrews 12:1 and fill in the blanks:
Therefore, since we are surrounded by such a great cloud of witnesses, let us_____ everything that hinders us and the sin that so easily _____ us.

David was on a mission, heading to the front lines for his family. After he arrives on the battlefield, before he moves forward, he leaves his baggage with the Baggage Keeper.

Are you willing to leave your baggage of guilt at the cross of Jesus, your Baggage Keeper?

You can leave your baggage there and move forward, relying on the promises of Christ. You are forgiven. You are loved. You are not alone. You have a plan and a purpose.

Select your favorite verse from Day 1 then flip forward to Day 5 of this chapter and record it in the top box. For the rest of today spend time in prayer meditating and living out the verse you selected.

A Prayer

Heavenly Father, my Jehovah-Rapha, the Lord Who Heals, my heart is heavy and broken. The weight on my shoulders is overwhelming. I feel weak and doubtful, but I long to be strong and confident. Help me lay my burdens and my baggage down once and for all. Some days, in my hurting, I fight against You. Forgive me, Lord. I ask for Your tender grace to help me lean on You at my side for my support and understanding. Please re-create in me a passion for more of You as I learn to lay my guilt and shame down at Your feet. May today be a new day of victory. In the strong name of Jesus Christ I pray, Amen.

Day 2: Behind the Scenes and Hidden

Dr. Kathryn Butler: Juggling Guilt and Gifts

Where were you on April 15, 2013? For most of the world, it was another Monday. If you were like Dr. Kathryn Butler, you were at home. A trauma and critical care surgeon in Boston, she was taking a final day off to enjoy the last moments with her newborn son. Spending one more day with her newborn baby boy was the least she could do to make up for the future demands of her career.[4]

April 15, 2013, marked the running of the Boston Marathon where terrorists detonated two homemade bombs, killing three spectators and severely wounding more than 260 others. Kathryn Butler's hospital treated the majority of the wounded, and she knew nothing about it until hours after the bombing had occurred.

> As a specially trained caretaker and doctor, Dr. Butler felt overwhelmed by guilt. She should have been there to do her job, the job she'd trained for, the job she felt called to do.
>
> In a beautiful article, Dr. Butler said, "In my earnest desire for one more day at home with my baby, I'd inadvertently abandoned my colleagues. The realization sickened me."[5]

Have family obligations ever caused you to miss important events at work? Explain.

_____

_____

_____

When was the last time you disappointed your coworkers, teammates, or family members?

_____

_____

_____

She couldn't have known her anguish was only beginning. Not being present at the hospital during the bombing's aftermath was the least of the guilt she would experience. Over the following days and weeks, Dr. Butler had to choose between her son's care and caring for hundreds of injured people.

Can you relate to Dr. Kathryn Butler's conflict and feelings of guilt?

_____

What's your biggest struggle with regrets and feelings of guilt?

_____

Dr. Kathryn Butler was left struggling with her choices in the aftermath of the Boston bombing. She believed she had a calling to be a trauma surgeon, to work the long hours, to do what God had designed her to do, but she was also called to raise her son. What's the right choice? Is there an answer?

Summarize the following passages:
Romans 12:6-8

Romans 11:29

> "... When we acknowledge our own brokenness and lean into His faithfulness, even anxieties that steal our breath can bless us." – Dr. Kathryn Butler

Jochebed: Facing Personal Crisis

We've already read a little about David in 1 Samuel, but let's look behind the scenes of another great hero of the Old Testament: Moses. Moses' story begins with his mother, **Jochebed**.

You can find Jochebed's story in Exodus 2:1-10, a passage packed full of behind-the-scenes stories, if you read between the lines. Look it up and check it out. Talk about crazy.

Jochebed lived during a time in Egyptian history when the Hebrews, her people, were slaves. Due to the vast size of their population, Pharaoh and other leaders were afraid of a revolt, because if the Hebrews had turned against them, they would have been completely outnumbered. So the Pharaoh came up with a truly evil plan to murder every newborn boy (found in Exodus 1).

Try to imagine yourself in Jochebed's place. Soldiers march down from the capital and break into homes, snatching babies from their cribs and flinging them into the raging waters of the Nile River. Mothers were forced to watch, helpless.

But Jochebed was different. She believed her little boy was special, and she hid him from the soldiers. Not for a week, but for **three whole months**.

But eventually she couldn't hide him in their home anymore, so she made a basket of papyrus reeds and waterproofed it with tar. Then, she put her baby in the basket and hid him in the reeds of the Nile, and she left him there with only his sister to watch over him from a distance.

Ever since my high school and college years, I have been involved in musical theater, so I love to think behind the scenes, to imagine what life must have been like for Jochebed's family during those three months. Jochebed had to avoid the soldiers and conversations with her friends and neighbors about her baby. She had to make her other children do the same. And every time she overheard the sorrow and heartbreak of her friends who had lost their children, how guilty she must have felt because her son was still alive.

Jochebed would have gone down to the river to wash clothes for the family. Maybe she could see where her son's basket was hidden. Other babies his age would be learning to lift their heads, experiencing the tastes and smells of life, but not her son. He was stuck in a basket in the water. How could he ever have a normal life? How could she call herself a good mother?

And what would have happened if soldiers had found him? They would have killed him, yes, but it would have been a death sentence for her entire family too. She had to wonder if she'd done the right thing.

Read Exodus 2:5-9. What happened?

_____

_____

Did the princess know the baby wasn't Egyptian? Why do you think it didn't matter to her?

_____

_____

How do you think Jochebed felt when her daughter came to tell her the news?

_____

_____

Jochebed entrusted her child to God's care in the most terrifying of circumstances. Now don't start thinking Jochebed had it all together. Nobody does. But we do know Jochebed was brave. She was brave enough to do what God asked her to do no matter what it was.

So what happened to Jochebed? It's important to know how her story unfolded because we can learn a valuable lesson when God doesn't work the way we expect.

Jochebed had received her baby boy back into her arms, safe and sound. She could nurse him, raise him, care for him freely, and in the moment, she had to be so happy because she trusted God. But her story wasn't finished because Pharaoh's daughter came back.

Read Exodus 2:10. How would you feel if you were Jochebed?

_____

What do you think was God's purpose in this limited time raising Moses?

_____

Well, we know the full story. We know who Moses is and who he grew to become. We know his amazing accomplishments. We know the plan God had for him, but Jochebed didn't. Surely she had to wonder if she had done the right thing.

The more we read Scripture, the more we see how every God-follower in history has ended up in a situation where their strength runs out. Every situation is different and unique. What you are struggling with right now is completely different from someone else is experiencing, but one thing you can know for sure: We are all struggling to do what God has called us to do, and we can't do it without His help.

Some of us are plagued with guilt whenever we think we are failing, falling short, or being ineffective. Guilt is a heavy burden to bear, and many times we experience it the most when we make choices we know aren't good for us. This might be guilt over not taking care of our physical needs like eating and exercise, guilt over being impatient and critical, or guilt over what we wish we could change from our past.

"Nothing paralyzes our lives like the attitude that things can never change. We need to remind ourselves

that God can change things. Outlook determines outcome. If we see only the problems, we will be defeated; but if we see the possibilities in the problems, we can have victory." – Warren Wiersbe

I believe God can and will help us turn our feelings of guilt and shame around in a positive way. Grace from God is a gift to every believer. Instead of living with our guilty feelings, let's choose to live on God's truth and grace.

Instead of focusing on the guilt you feel or searching for God's permission for your heart's desires, why not look for verses celebrating who God is and what He does for us?

What can you learn about God from the following verses?
Isaiah 43:25

_____

John 1:14

_____

John 15:4-5

_____

2 Corinthians 12:8-9

_____

1 Timothy 2:1-5

_____

Following Jesus is a never-ending adventure. He calls us to walk with Him down paths that transform us, journeys that make us into something different than we started.

Select your favorite verse from Day 2 then flip forward to Day 5 of this chapter and record it in the top box. For the rest of today spend time in prayer meditating and living out the verse you selected.

A Prayer

Dear Lord Jesus, You are Faithful and True. I believe You are King of kings and Lord of lords. Please help me to truly accept

Your grace and love for me. I'm still dealing with my feelings of "not being good enough." Shame is not from You and can be powerfully crippling. I'm crying out to You and trusting You to work in my life for good. As I begin this journey of healing, use me to pass on to others the grace I'm receiving from You. Only You can move mountains, and I believe You will do it. Amen.

Day 3: Are You Heading in the Right Direction?

Have you noticed your duffle bag gets heavier and bigger with every passing year? When you were young, your backpack was cool, but as you grew up, you had to carry more stuff with you. Your duffle bag doesn't get lighter or smaller over time. It's like you still have a million knick-knacks to carry around.

It's so heavy and so awkward, and you can't exactly give it to someone else to carry for you. It's your stuff, but it weighs you down and makes life more difficult than it should be. But you can't let go. You need your stuff.

Sound familiar?

Guilt is a horrible thing to feel, and it pounds away at us because of our pasts, our unreasonable expectations, and the relentless blame from people around us. The worst trouble with this kind of guilt is how easily we can hide it. We can tuck it away where no one can see it and keep functioning from day to day. But just because no one can see it doesn't mean it's not there, causing terrible damage.

Christian author Randy Alcorn categorizes guilt in two ways: Residual and False.

Residual guilt stems from not accepting God's forgiveness. We can believe we have it without truly accepting it. It's like being given a Christmas gift but never opening it. It's refusing to believe God actually forgives, even though the Bible assures us He does.[6]

What do you discover about God's forgiveness from the following verses? Jeremiah 31:34

Micah 7:19

False guilt is blaming ourselves or accepting punishment for actions or results we never committed. We imagine ourselves as the ones to blame, even if we have no responsibility for what happened. This type of guilt is rampant in our world, stemming from perfectionism or experiences at home, school, work, or church.[7]

> **"You can sit there forever, lamenting about how bad you've been, feeling guilty until you die, and not one tiny slice of guilt will do anything to change a single thing in the past. Move on." - Wayne Dyer**

Do you identify with any of these real-life people and their stories of guilt?

Millennial: Greg/ 29/ Single "I'm so tired of hiding from everyone at work and at church. No one knows I'm struggling with drugs, and I feel so guilty playing the church game. And to top it off, my family keeps pressing me to get married. I'm such a mess right now, I can't be in a serious relationship. Isn't there anyone I can be honest about my life with?"

Millennial: Elizabeth/ 31/ No kids/ Married 1 year "I haven't been able to travel to all the places I've dreamed about yet. I already feel guilty for wanting to delay starting our family. I'm just not ready to give my new business up and call it quits. I'm just starting, and I really like what I'm doing. I know God has given me favor and gifts to do this business. What do I do with all this internal guilt?"

X-ennial: Brooke/ 35/ Single "I've made so many mistakes. I feel so guilty. I know God says to ask, seek, and receive forgiveness and hope, but my heart still struggles with fear. I read blogs, listen to Podcasts, go to church, even attend a Bible study—so why isn't this working? Why don't I see answers to my prayers?"

Generation X: Dawn/ 4 Kids/ Married "I'm so broken. I have felt guilty my entire life, and I don't know why. I say I'm sorry to everyone about everything. I know as a Christian it isn't right, but I can't seem to rise above the guilt I feel. There's no hope for me. I believe in answered prayers for others, just not for me."

Generation X: Adam/ 45/ Widower I'm so angry with God for letting my wife die. How did I miss the signs of her illness? I feel so guilty, like a lousy husband, like I failed her. I'm falling and need someone to catch me, and I don't know if I can trust God to help me. I just can't face all these guilty feelings anymore. I don't know what to do."

Baby Boomer: Melanie/ 2 kids/ Divorced after 25 years "I feel so guilty. I swore I would never put my kids through a divorce like my parents put me through and look at me. It happened to me and now to them too. I have no retirement. I have to go back to full-time work, and I'm not really sure what I will do. I feel betrayed and guilty for my failed marriage. Only God can help me.

Which one of these stories resonates with you the most? Why?

_____

_____

Do you struggle with talking about yourself or your feelings of guilt? Why or why not?

_____

_____

> Let's pray right now. Silently, tell God what you feel. Tell Him the guilty thoughts invading your life. Let Him know what you're thinking.

Growing Spiritually Requires Obedience

My husband and I started our family in the busy years between my late 20s and mid-30s. I can't even tell you the joy my two sons and my daughter brought to my life, even when all three of them were under the age of five. During the same time in our lives, I owned a performing arts school where I taught around 400 students. I also volunteered at my church. I was blessed beyond measure, but my plate was overflowing.

Can you relate?
What's on your plate? What other parts of your life take up your time and focus?

_____

Do you think God has called you to do everything on your to-do list?

_____

What are you doing with the guilt you are feeling?

_____

_____

I was connected at my church. Being able to engage with a caring community made life brighter and opened doors for me to help other people. I felt fulfilled and satisfied, as though I could finally present myself as someone who was making a difference.

Instead, I felt God tugging on my heart and asking me to change my life. He made it very clear through Scriptures like Isaiah 48:17, sermons, readings, and prayer—He was moving me in a new direction: sell the business.

Has God ever given you directions you didn't want to follow? When?

_____

Share a story about a time God told you to do something crazy.

_____

_____

What did you do? What happened afterward?

_____

_____

What decisions are you facing currently? Circle as many as apply.

Job Decisions	Children's School / Extracurricular Activities	Financial Pressures
Strained Family Relationships		Unwanted Bad Habits

"God will never lead you where His strength cannot keep you." - Barbara Johnson

What was I doing wrong? This business I had built from the ground up, my students who trusted me, my students' parents who looked to me for help—God was asking me to walk away from it. You want to talk about guilt? How could I turn my back on part of my life? Was God punishing me because I hadn't put Him and my family first?

Slowly, day by day, I felt the peace coming to my heart. I didn't understand, and I didn't want to do it. But God was clear. This was what He wanted, so I did it, although I did it quietly. The business itself was inside a beautiful four-story building. We rented the first floor out to pay the mortgage, and I used the top three floors for the school. So when you entered, you had to walk up three flights of steps to the second floor.

Picture in your mind me, a woman carrying a diaper bag, a backpack, and a child on her hip, with two little ones in tow, climbing those stairs every morning. And on every step, we would all say a word from Philippians 4:13, my life verse I chose as my favorite and memorized with my family at the time.

What is a Bible verse you would like to memorize?

_____

I had a staircase for Philippians 4:13. Brainstorm some actions or motions you can use to help make memorizing verses easier.

_____

_____

_____

I continued to teach every afternoon, even though no one else knew my secret. It took three years for the business to sell. There were times during those three years I didn't know what to do. How could I sell the business without advertising it? What was God even doing in my life? There were times I would think: **"Hello, God. Are you up there? Do you see me?"**

Have you ever asked God if He can see you? _____

Well, shortly after the business sold, my husband got transferred to another city for a promotion at his job. Soon, God was moving our family to a new town in a new state.

Because God prepared me ahead of time, I'd been able to sell my business to someone who would take care of it, who would continue to invest in my precious community.

All those years, I'd struggled with guilt and uncertainty when I didn't have to, because God had a plan for my future. I had to be brave enough to do what He was asking me to do.

How about you? Are you hearing from God today? What are you specifically praying about right now?

_____

Select your favorite verse from Day 3 then flip forward to Day 5 of this chapter and record it in the top box. For the rest of today spend time in prayer meditating and living out the verse you selected.

A Prayer

Holy Spirit, my Advocate and Defender, what a gift to know You forgive me and love me no matter what fears and weaknesses I have hidden deep inside of me. Please move in my soul and help me grow strong. I surrender my brokenness. Today, I'm laying all of my worries at the foot of the cross. Please forgive me. I choose Your truth and the gift of forgiveness. I long to walk in victory every day with You at my side. In the name of my Rescuer and Protector, Jesus Christ, I pray, Amen.

Day 4: Path of Unwanted Thoughts

Are you tired of loud, complaining people on the phone or on social media? Do you feel distracted everywhere you go, whether you're sitting at home or driving your car? Has a distraction ever made you take a wrong turn on the highway? Maybe you took the wrong exit, and then you wasted hours trying to get back on track. Or maybe you got busy cleaning the house because company was coming to visit, and you missed a Very Important Phone Call.

Whatever happened, you disappointed someone, or maybe you disappointed yourself.

But whether your disappointment happened yesterday or even last week, we need to change our focus.

Sometimes we allow ourselves to think and focus on our past mistakes, mess-ups, and weaknesses. This pattern continually nurtures our guilt and shame and opens the door to *condemnation* from the enemy, rather than *conviction* from the Lord.

Knowing the difference between these two words will help us tear down the strongholds in our hearts and minds (a stronghold is a false thinking pattern of deception and lies; read more in 2 Corinthians 10:4).

CONDEMNATION → Shows you your past and shouts, "Loser."

CONVICTION → Shows you the solution and shouts, "Seek Jesus, who washes your sins away and gives you eternal forgiveness."

"God's Word acts as a light for our paths. It can help scare off unwanted thoughts in our minds and protect us from the enemy." – Gary Smalley and John Trent

Let's dig deeper into the nitty gritty about this problem of guilt we all struggle with.

What You Say About Yourself	Bible Verse to Look Up	What Does God Say?
I have to hide.	Psalm 32:2,5	
I am never good enough.	Ephesians 2:4,6	
There's no grace for me.	Isaiah 30:18	
I don't deserve mercy.	Micah 7:18-19	
I'm so guilty.	Isaiah 43:25	
I am condemned.	Romans 8:1	
God doesn't care	1 Peter 5:7	
My failures are unforgivable.	1 John 1:9	

False guilt can be hard to spot sometimes, and the only weapon we have against it is the truth. Knowing and believing the truth will stop false guilt in its tracks before it damages us or our most precious relationships.

Guilt and shame don't draw us closer to God. They push us away from Him. And anything that pushes us away from God doesn't come from Him. God will always be specific.

"When grace moves in … guilt moves out." - Max Lucado

The stronghold of guilt and shame you are living with today can be torn down. Talk to God. Spend time with Him. Ask Him to reveal His will for you today. Spend time talking with your mentor. Discuss these Scriptures and dig deeply into the character of God. Be brave enough to work through what He is leading you to do and remember you are never alone.

Write out and meditate on Philippians 4:8 below:

_____

_____

Talk to Him. Spend time with Him. Ask Him to reveal His will for you today. Does He want you in the workforce? Does He want you to stay home?

If you belong to Jesus, something amazing is taking place in your life. Look up 2 Corinthians 3:16-18 and write down what God says is happening to you.

_____

_____

Select your favorite verse from Day 4 then flip forward to Day 5 of this chapter and record it in the top box. For the rest of today spend time in prayer meditating and living out the verse you selected.

A Prayer

Dear God, Jehovah-Shalom, the Lord of Peace, I love You. I'm coming to You with all my heart and soul. Take me as I am, the good and the messy parts. Right now, I lay my hurts and guilty feelings at Your feet. Take them from me, Lord Jesus. Help me to have victory over my negative thoughts. Transform my thought life into a life filled with Your peace and grace. Break this stronghold over my mind and heart. I long to live in the freedom You give all Your children. I want to live life like the child of the King. In the mighty name of my King Lord Jesus. Amen.

Day 5: The Path to Guilt-Free Living

As you complete each daily section of this study, write down your favorite verse from each day.

Day 1: _____

Day 2: _____

Day 3: _____

Day 4: _____

Choosing to trust that God keeps His promises is the biggest step you can take to living guilt-free. And one of the greatest promises He's made to you and to me can be found in Colossians 2:13-14.

Find this passage and write it here word for word:

_____

_____

The record, the history, of our sins—our guilt—was erased when Jesus died for us. Our condemning flaws and failures are no longer part of our story. God took them away.

Guilt and shame are burdens you were never designed to carry. Would you leave them at His cross? Write down the feelings of guilt you are experiencing in the space provided below and give them all to Jesus today.

Journaling the Journey

1. Begin to select your life verse. There are more than 31,000 verses to pick from. Write a few of your favorites here and pray about your selection. Then, write it in the space provided.

_____

_____

_____

_____

_____

A - Adore the Lord. Tell God who you acknowledge He is. I like to go through the alphabet to help me stay focused. (i.e. God you are Awesome. I love Your beautiful creation. You are the Creator God and I Delight in You. etc…)

C - Confess your sin. Be very specific.

T - Thanksgiving. Only say what you are thankful for and nothing else.

S – Supplication. Here is where you ask God for your needs and the needs of others.

2. What's stopping you from allowing God to take your guilt and shame away?

_____

_____

_____

_____

_____

_____

_____

_____

_____

_____

_____

_____

_____

_____

_____

_____

_____

_____

3. Write a prayer to God, using the ACTS acronym.

_____

_____

_____

_____

_____

_____

_____

_____

_____

_____

A Prayer

Dear Lord Jesus, You are my Bread of Life and my Sustainer. I'm humbled in the presence of Your mighty, awesome power. Increase Your grace and open my eyes to see the lies, deception, ugly words, and untruths I've allowed into my life. Guide me to resist the pull on my life into the strongholds the enemy has set up for me. Help me grow strong and mature in my new faith commitment to You today. Thank You for Your grace. Show me a better way to experience the joy of living with You by my side. May I find favor in Your eyes all the days of my life. In the name of Jesus I pray, Amen.

> **Mentoring Tip: Put to rest your feelings of guilt and shame with help from your Mentor leading you to the forgiveness of Christ at the cross.**

CONVERSATION 3

Does God Love Others More Than Me?

Turning his head Peter noticed the disciple Jesus loved following right behind. When Peter noticed him, he asked Jesus, "Master, what's going to happen to him?" Jesus said, "If I want him to live until I come again, what's that to you? You—follow Me." John 21:20-22 (MSG)

Day 1: But What About Me?

"Envy is a universal threat to our joy." – John Piper

It happened when you went to pick up a set of concert tickets from a friend's house. You walked in the front door and spied the neatly organized living room without a single junk pile anywhere. Nothing was out of place. Maybe the cool wall hangings caught your eye, or perhaps you marveled at the tastefully arranged flowers in the vase on the table. Before you could stop yourself, you thought: *I could never decorate like they do. I will never invite anyone to my house. I'd be so embarrassed for them to see how I live.*

It's true. Some people keep a tidy house or can make beautiful decorations out of scraps, but knowing how to arrange flowers doesn't mean they have the rest of their lives sorted out. Can you relate to this feeling? You walk in the room, but your joy and heart's satisfaction with God goes out the door?

You are not alone. It happened to Peter too. In John 21, Peter has been restored, and Jesus has been in a conversation with him, face to face. But right in the middle of the conversation, Peter wants to know, "What about John?" Peter should have been joyful about the positive attention and one-on-one conversation with Jesus. Instead, his joy is distracted by his envy of the younger disciple, John.

What is envy? Webster's Dictionary defines envy as "the painful or resentful awareness of an advantage enjoyed by another, joined with a desire to possess the same advantage." (Merriam-Webster's Collegiate Dictionary, 10th ed.)

Envy is everywhere. Most of us participate unaware, so if you catch yourself looking at others and sizing them up, don't think you're the only one who does it. We heap stress upon stress on our shoulders, desiring to measure up to an impossible, invisible standard set by the people we admire. Maybe you think you're a failure when you have those competitive or envious thoughts, and you think there's something wrong with you. There isn't.

Most people have something about themselves they wish were different, whether it's their appearance or their job, their marital status or their kids' achievements. Envy has a root in dissatisfaction, insecurities, and a lack of identity in Christ. When we read Proverbs 14:30, we can see how God encourages us to exchange our envy for His love.

Write Proverbs 14:30 below and highlight the key words you see.

_____

_____

Constantly competing with others will eventually steal your joy. It takes your focus off what matters and leads you to devalue yourself, your God-given gifts, and your blessings from God.

So how do you escape the self-destructive trap of envy? The key is knowing your triggers.

What triggers the emotions of insecurity?

_____

What starts those internal hurricanes of doubt and paralyzing fear?

_____

What's holding you back from becoming a fully satisfied, confident follower of Christ?

_____

Did you realize three out of ten adults worry they've disappointed the people closest to them in their lives?[8] And don't think the danger is only outside the church. Church-going Christians are as susceptible to envy as others.

What are Christians thinking?[9]

Let's dig deeper into Colossians 3:2. Using your Bible resources or a Bible app, look up this verse in three different translations of the Bible. Your choice.

(_____) _____

(_____) _____

(_____) _____

God wants to reveal what is distracting and discouraging you and what makes you sad instead of joy-filled. Let's find out together.

Select your favorite verse from Day 1 then flip forward to Day 5 of this chapter and record it in the top box. For the rest of today spend time in prayer meditating and living out the verse you selected.

A Prayer

Heavenly Father, I want to trust You with all of my heart. But I've tried this before and failed. Show me the way to change. I've been caught in the trap of envy and competition with others for way too long. I desire to have a fully-satisfied heart. Help me be content with who I am in You. The envy in my heart is ugly and needs to come to an end. I know I need to die to myself and live for Christ. But how do I do it? Lord, help me. I want to change. Help me stay on the path of contentment and satisfaction in You. I accept Your plan for my life and pray for guidance along the way. In the name of Jesus, Amen.

Day 2: God First, Others Second, I'm Third
Shawn Johnson: Before and After

Do you remember being 16? For some of us, 16 was comfortable. Some of us were surrounded by friends and family members. Some of us had a supportive and encouraging community. The future was full of possibilities.

But what if you had experienced the greatest moment of your life when you were 16? What if you became a household name? What if you were called America's Sweetheart? What if you had to carry the expectations and dreams of an entire country on your shoulders when you weren't even old enough to drive?

What area of your faith do you desire to be stretched and grow?

Shawn Johnson was 16 years old at the 2008 Summer Olympics where she won the gold medal for the balance beam in gymnastics, but for the individual all-around competition, she lost the gold to her teammate and roommate Nastia Lukin. But she still won silver. A silver medal at the Olympics should have been worth celebrating, right?

> **"I felt like I had failed the world," Johnson said. "I felt like since the world saw me as nothing else, that if I failed at being a gymnast, I had failed at being a human being."[10]**

Then, during the medal presentation ceremony, the person who slipped the silver medal around her neck said two cutting words to her: "I'm sorry."

What would you have felt in Shawn Johnson's place?

How would that feeling have changed your perception of yourself?

Shawn Johnson had wanted a gold medal for herself as a champion. Instead, her friend won it, and the emotional need to compete with her friend filled her heart. Johnson, who doesn't have the stereotypical body shape of a perfect gymnast according to the media, was always held up against her friend Nastia Lukin.

"The best and most beautiful things in the world cannot be seen or even touched. They must be felt with the heart." – Helen Keller

I wonder if Shawn Johnson knew how much of a blessing she would be to the world, and I'm not talking about her gold and silver medals or her championships from "Dancing with the Stars." Because there's more to Shawn Johnson than her Olympic and professional victories.

Due to the tremendous amount of shaming the media heaped on her while she was in the spotlight, Johnson teamed up with Dove, the soap manufacturer, in a campaign designed to redefine the concept of beauty in the world.[11] Instead of giving in to the talking heads about what she should look like or what she should be wearing, Johnson is pressing forward and leading the way for girls around the world to have confidence in their appearances, to embrace the way they were made.

Beyond her work with self-image, Johnson has been gut-level honest with the world in her recent struggle with a miscarriage, sharing the very personal videos exchanged between her and her husband.[12] Talk about courageous. She had a willingness to put herself out in front of the world, to strip her soul bare and not hold anything back about who she is, what she's struggling with, and how she feels, and she did it so others like her would know they weren't alone.

Could you tell your story of pain and tragedy if you knew it would help someone else?

God has a purpose for your life. Remember, everyone experiences pain and tragedy. Don't believe the Instagram-filter life of social media where someone can look cheerful and happy when in reality their life has a few bumps in the road too.

Take a moment and ask God to give you a crystal-clear vision of your life and His purpose for you. He hears you, and He always answers.

Leah: From Dad to Daughter to Disappointment

Let's talk about a woman named Leah. Take a moment to read her story in Genesis 29:15-35. Leah was the oldest daughter of a shepherd named Laban, and she had every reason to envy her younger sister Rachel.

The story actually begins several chapters earlier with a set of twin boys named Jacob and Esau. Genesis, the first book in the Bible, is basically the history of one family. This one family would eventually become the nation of Israel, but when the family started it was just a family like anyone else's. Jacob and Esau were the third generation, and they'd had a terrible falling out. The story of their relationship is in Genesis 27, but what you need to know is Jacob was on the run. He'd left his mother and father's tent to find a wife with his uncle Laban's family. And Jacob found Rachel.

Do you have a sibling you envy?

_____

Is there a person at church or work who makes you struggle with anger or envy?

_____

Describe this scenario.

_____

_____

_____

Let's look at Genesis 29:16-17.
How does the Bible describe Leah?

_____

_____

How does the Bible describe Rachel?

_____

_____

Are you telling yourself the truth? Do you need to replace your negative thinking with truth from God's Word? *Look up and read what God Says about you in the Scriptures.*

I Think	God Says
I'm not special.	You are My masterpiece. Ephesians 2:10
My body is embarrassing.	I created you, and you are wonderful. Psalm 139
There's no hope for me to change.	I am here. There is always hope. Psalm 73:24
I feel so invisible.	Remember, I see you. Matthew 9:22
I'm not attractive enough.	You are beautiful to Me. Psalm 45:11

In the story, Jacob volunteers to work for his uncle for seven years to earn the right to marry Rachel. Rachel must have been gorgeous, because Jacob wasn't a dummy. Jacob was brilliant, a schemer, a planner, and this girl made him lose his mind. He really did love her, and as far as we know, Rachel loved him back.

Scripture encourages us to be concerned with inner beauty, not our outward appearance. I'm so glad God is looking at the inside of a person. 1 Samuel 16:7 says "the Lord looks at the heart."

> **"There is an art to differentiating between goals and desires. A goal is an outcome that requires only my cooperation to achieve, and a desire is an outcome that requires the cooperation of another person to be achieved." – Larry Crabb**

So what's the problem? Read Genesis 29:20-25.
How do you think Leah felt about all this?

_____

_____

How do you think Jacob's reaction made her feel about herself?

_____

_____

Share about a time when you were caught between two people and you didn't feel like you measured up. What did you do? How did you reconcile? Or did you?

_____

_____

Once Jacob had married both Leah and Rachel, life only got more complicated. Of course it would with two wives. Can you imagine? But if Leah felt envious of Rachel before, it would have been worse now.

Rachel was beautiful. She was vibrant. She sparkled. And she was cherished. She was everything Leah wasn't. Can't you see Leah working extra hard to prepare a meal to impress her husband? Maybe she spent time and energy trying to make herself look beautiful so Jacob would notice her. Maybe she gave him gifts so he might see her as his wife too.

But no matter what Leah did, Jacob would never love her like he loved Rachel. Leah's goal was to be loved by Jacob, but this goal would only lead to disappointment. Achieving her goal depended on Jacob.

Have you ever set a goal or had a dream that required someone else to cooperate to reach a successful end? Explain.

_____

_____

How can you change your goal so you're the only one responsible for it? Rewrite it here.

_____

_____

Certainly Leah had to feel alone. Unloved and unlovely, she had to feel abandoned and rejected, like Jacob had validated how worthless she'd always felt. And it's as wrong now as it was then.

Leah had a difficult life. The fact is, everyone deals with disappointments along the way. But God will always show up in our toughest times. Even though she was the least favorite wife, God blessed Leah with the most children and called her to have a leading parental role for the blended family. God blessed Leah as a prominent mother of the 12 Tribes of Israel, and her children were used in the ongoing history of God's people.

She was the mother of Judah, through whom the line of Jesus, our Savior, would come. Though God was with the members of this blended family, they would have to face multiple challenges during their journey with Him. God chose to exchange Leah's troubles and sorrows for blessings.

If you have a blended family of his-and-hers children, what are the challenges you struggle with today?

_____

_____

What situations do you need to work through on your special family gatherings?

_____

_____

List a few ways you could help your family members to not compete with each other.

_____

_____

Select your favorite verse from Day 2 then flip forward to Day 5 of this chapter and record it in the top box. For the rest of today spend time in prayer meditating and living out the verse you selected.

A Prayer

Dear Lord Jesus, Thank You for loving me for who I am. You have created all of us uniquely and differently. Help me to remember I am loved, and You have written my name on the palms of Your hands. Thank You for being my Rescuer and gentle Provider. I long to live in a place where I will fully trust You. With You at my side I will learn to rest in Your plan for my life and not my own. Thank You ahead of time for giving me the strength to keep my eyes on Your unfailing goodness and extravagant mercies. I don't know what to do, so my eyes are on You and You alone, Amen.

"When you're suffering, remember nothing happens to you that is unnoticed by God. He sees and understands everything that goes on in your life."
– Elizabeth George

Day 3: Ordinary Me, Extraordinary God

Can you see the hand of God when you hold a young child in your arms? I can remember as a young tween holding my baby sister and marveling at the softness of her little hands and tiny feet. Squirming, wriggling, crying—the tiny little life in your hands was born to change the world, and God has a plan for their lives like He has a plan and purpose for you and me.

Every time I hold one of my kids—or now my grandkids—or someone else's kids at the nursery, God's truth is so real to me. He creates His children and provides them the breath, love, and comfort they need.

Whether you are a single woman walking in faith or a woman waiting on God to start your family, we all know how precious children are to God.

For you created my inmost being; you knit me together in my mother's womb. I praise you because I am fearfully and wonderfully made; your works are wonderful, I know that full well. Psalm 139:13-14

Blessed are the peacemakers, for they will be called children of God. Matthew 5:9

But Jesus called the children to him and said, "Let the little children come to me, and do not hinder them, for the kingdom of God belongs to such as these. Luke 18:16

I finally saw a small picture of God's love for me through my kids.

Let me explain: Before I met my first born, Jered, I already decided I loved him. I didn't care what he looked like or if he loved me in return. I knew he was God's creation and a gift for my husband and me to love. There was nothing anyone could do or say to change my mind. I loved Jered with all of my heart and soul before he was even born, and the same was true with my other two kids.

This is how God loves you and me, only much more than we can wrap our minds around. God is the Creator of all life and loves every human being before they are even conceived.

You see, I totally believe in Elohim, my Creator God.

ELOHIM is the first name for God found in the Bible, and it's used throughout the Old Testament more than 2,300 times. Elohim comes from the Hebrew root meaning "strength" or "power" and has the unusual characteristic of being plural in form. In Genesis 1:1, we read:

"In the beginning Elohim created the heaven and the earth." Right from the start, this plural form for the name of God is used to describe the One God, a mystery to be uncovered throughout the rest of the Bible.

I believe with all my heart God hears our prayers and has our best interests in His plan, because He cares about His creation. I am convinced and determined to share with others how God is love and loves to answer prayers. If you continue to walk in unbelief in God's power to show up, answer prayers, and move in miraculous ways on a daily basis you will begin to feel defeated and discouraged.

Be encouraged my friend. 2 Chronicles 16:9 says, "The eyes of the Lord search the whole earth in order to strengthen those whose hearts are fully committed to him."

Do you believe this scripture?

_____

What is your biggest struggle with prayer right now?

_____

What is your focus when you try to pray? Choose One:
Doubt   Limitations   Too risky   Anticipation   Hope   Confidence

I prayed to God for sons. This mattered so much to me because I had two brothers, Eddie and Walter, but I never got the chance to know them. Eddie died of a brain tumor when I was four months old. Two years and four months later, Walter died too, suffering from a rare heart condition.

I missed seeing them grow up, fall in love, and have families of their own. I felt like I missed a blessing. So I prayed for two healthy boys, but I fixed my eyes on "boys" and gave the end result to God.

My family suffered a lot of trauma, a lot of joy and pain like every other family in the world. After the deaths of my brothers, my parents clung to my older sister Sandy and me as their lifelines, and they looked for comfort and peace in the church. Four years later, my little sister SuAnne came along, and we celebrated like we'd never celebrated before. I'm sure you can understand why.

God is with us in the good and bad times. He desires for us to choose to run to Him and not run away during times of testing or triumph.

What areas of your life challenge your trust in God?

_____

_____

How can you grow in your faith to trust God and His promises during the tough times?

_____

_____

Write your thoughts here and then pray for God's wisdom and plan to discuss this with your mentor.

_____

_____

Two years later, our second son, Jason, was born, and we were so grateful. But God, our Producer/Director, decided our family wasn't complete. God gave us our third child, baby Joanna. I signed my name as MOTHER for a third time with a heart full of thanksgiving and praise, and our final production number (as I like to call her) as our family was complete.

My heart was full, but my sleep tank was empty.

My kids didn't sleep. So neither did I. Anxieties plagued me. Why aren't they sleeping? Is lack of sleep going to hurt them in the future? Will they fail to be productive members of society if they don't get a restorative night's sleep as an infant?

With three kids so close in age, it didn't take me long to be at the end of my rope. I needed help; I needed balance in my life. How could I be a good wife, mom, teacher, leader, and friend? I couldn't.

Before I knew it, the guilt in my heart started to grow, and I was overwhelmed emotionally. No matter where I looked, it seemed like all the other moms weren't struggling like I was. I became envious of them, and it wasn't a pretty picture. I finally reached out to my mentor and reconnected with her. I made my mentoring relationship a priority and became encouraged and calm inside my soul again. My blessings came when my mentor poured into me on a weekly basis and led me to the truth in God's Word. She helped me see God's hand in my life and His love for me and my family. She lovingly helped me to see my heart as it really was. We prayed against the envy and strife in my life and asked the Lord to give me a new heart.

Did you know God's Word mentions envy and strife together several times? Let's look at two verses.

- Romans 1:29
- 1 Timothy 6:4

The turning point in my life happened when I sought God and shared my expectations with my mentor. She became my sounding board and listened to my heart as I poured out my concerns and fears.

Her God-stories blessed me. She was able to encourage me and share how she saw God working in her life and mine. She made mistakes too. She had disappointments, but her godly advice and wisdom to focus on God and His Word gave me hope and peace.

Can you recall a relative, neighbor, schoolteacher, coach, or Sunday school teacher who made an investment in your life? Sometimes a mentoring relationship can be happening right in front of us without us realizing it. Who was this special person in your life? Describe the situation.

_____

_____

What was the biggest blessing in your life from this experience?

_____

As you meet in your mentoring relationship in the near future, what topics are on the top of your list and on your heart today?

_____

> Put your pen or pencil down and tell God how thankful you are for the people who encourage you.

The key to my positive life change is the counsel I received from my mentors over the years to continuously count my blessings, thanking the Lord for my blessings in prayer.

Are you willing to count it all joy? Here is James 1:2-4 (NLT). Circle every *you* and *your* to take ownership of the blessing:

> Dear brothers and sisters when troubles of any kind come your way, consider it an opportunity for great joy. For you know that when your faith is tested, your endurance has a chance to grow. So let it grow, for when your endurance is fully developed, you will be perfect and complete, needing nothing.

I was strongly encouraged to write my blessings in a journal and tell others what God was doing in my life. This counsel comes from Scripture.

Read the following Scriptures and circle the one you need today.

1 Chronicles 16:8-11, 23-24 Psalm 71:15-24 Isaiah 63:7

Select your favorite verse from Day 3 then flip forward to Day 5 of this chapter and record it in the top box. For the rest of today spend time in prayer meditating and living out the verse you selected.

A Prayer

Holy Spirit, I come to You with a broken heart and humbly ask You to show me the way to healing. You know all about my hurts and doubts. You know me better than anyone else and how I long to be satisfied with life. Touch me in a new and fresh way. I long to feel Your holy touch and hear Your gentle voice speaking into my soul. Help me trust You with my disappointment, fears, and discontentment. Plant Your joy again in my heart and give me a new song to sing. Only You can fill the hole in my heart. I pray all of this in the incredible, loving, strong name of Jesus Christ my Savior, Amen.

"Joy is the serious business of heaven." C.S. Lewis

Day 4: Envy vs. God's Grace

Soccer practice. Orchestra rehearsal. Mowing the lawn. Customer call. School play. House cleaning. Sick family member. Project management meeting. Vaccinations. Birthday party. Volleyball tournament. Changing the oil in the truck. Graduation. Work evaluation. Doctor's appointment. Grocery shopping. Aging parents.

You can't do it all. But you still try.

So what happens when you fail? What do you do when you try to accomplish the impossible and can't do it? It's not because you didn't try, but because accomplishing everything the people in your life ask you to do would require more than 24 hours and at least six arms.

God created you. God knows you by name. God sees your full life, schedule, past, present, and loves you the same. He made you and extends His grace to you unreservedly.

"Grace is God acting in our lives to do what we cannot do on our own." – Dallas Willard

Let's look at what God's grace really is:

> The Grace of God acknowledges the entire extent of my sin and still shows no condemnation.

Sometimes it is easier to show others grace than it is to give it to ourselves. If we really want to have a mature relationship with Christ, then we must drop our religious masks and be authentic. The Grace of God creates an environment of authenticity. God's grace helps us drop our mask and melt the envy away to reveal a pure heart full of trust and love.

Let's dig into Hebrews 4:16 to be encouraged and inspired. Highlight the key words.

"Let us, therefore, come boldly to the throne of grace, that we may obtain mercy and find grace to help us in our time of need."

In John 1:14-18, we learn Jesus came to this Earth for us, so we could have a life full of His grace and truth.

"Grace is not reserved for good people; grace underscores the goodness of God." – Andy Stanley

Let's take a look at why people live a life of envy instead of a life of grace. The truth is, one of the roots of envy is **fear**. We fear we won't measure up or we'll miss an opportunity we could have had. So instead of focusing on our blessings and the positives, our hearts focus on what has gone wrong and the negatives associated with it.

The trouble isn't just in the world either. You can struggle with envy within the church as often as you do out in the world. Sometimes we struggle with bringing the best dessert for Lifegroup, our kids' appearances on Sunday morning, or the people who look all together week in and week out. Within the church, we measure ourselves against each other. We don't want to admit it, but we envy our brothers and sisters in Christ. God never intended for us to see each other like this.

One of the greatest deterrents of envy is love. A well-known chapter in the Bible is 1 Corinthians 13, often called "The Love Chapter." It's a beautiful statement on what love really is and what it looks like.

> Read all of 1 Corinthians 13. Then, study verse 4 and fill in the blanks.
>
> 1. It does not _____.
> 2. It does not _____.
> 3. It is not _____.

Look up the verses in the chart below and write the letter next to the verse reference next to the corresponding message in the second column. Then, circle the verses you need today.

A. 1 Samuel 16:7   _____ You are never alone.

B. Matthew 6:6   _____ You are chosen.

C. Matthew 28:20   _____ God will equip you.

D. John 15:16   _____ God will supply all your needs.

E. Philippians 4:19   _____ God will complete the work he has started in you.

F. Philippians 1:6   _____ God sees your heart.

G. Hebrews 13:21   _____ God rewards you in secret.

Pray right now and ask God to silence the constant fears churning in your heart, so you can hear Him better.

The worst casualty of jealousy and envy is the relationship a person might have had with someone else. When you allow your heart to become full of envy, it's more difficult to be a friend and have special friendships. It's almost impossible to work together toward a common goal of love and compassion for others when envy is present. And working together is what God wants.

Look up the following verses and write down what God says about working together:
1 Corinthians 3:8

_____

1 Peter 3:8-9

_____

Envy is an issue of the heart. It can stem from fear, discontentment, and insecurity. Envy is extremely damaging to your relationship with the people around you. But fortunately God has given us a guidebook to help us defeat the green-eyed monster once and for all.

Look up the following verses and share a few words about what you are learning today:
Philippians 4:11-13

_____

Colossians 3:1-4

_____

Titus 2:11-14

_____

1 Timothy 6:6

_____

Select your favorite verse from Day 4 then flip forward to Day 5 of this chapter and record it in the top box. For the rest of today spend time in prayer meditating and living out the verse you selected.

A Prayer

Dear God, I know You are sitting on the throne, and You are alive and active in my life. I am learning all over again I can't do life without You. I'm so grateful to have You at my side. Forgive me for trying to do this journey by myself. You are my heart's desire. You are God, and I am not. You are the Author of Faith, the Bread of Life, and my Comforter. Help me to see You in new ways as I grow to become the godly person You created me to be. Today I remember who You are. You alone are enough for me. May I always seek Your will and plan for my life, Amen.

"Today you will envy the blessings of another, or you will bask in the wonder of the amazing grace you have been given." – Paul David Tripp

Day 5: From Broken to Whole in Christ

As you complete each daily section of this study, write down your favorite verse from each day.

```
Day 1: _____
Day 2: _____
Day 3: _____
Day 4: _____
```

Journaling the Journey

1. To help you fight envy and strife, write out the following verses in the spaces provided:

Isaiah 64:8 (I am the work of God's hand.)

_____

_____

Ephesians 2:10 (I am God's handiwork.)

_____

_____

2. Write down several ways God has personally blessed you in the past year.

_____

_____

3. Write a thank you prayer to the Lord for His grace and mercy.

_____

_____

A Prayer

Dear Lord Jesus, today I will set my eyes on the power of prayer and Your promises. Please set me free from all of my envy and strife. Show me Your path in every decision and guide me to apply Your Word to my life. I want to believe it is possible to change. Help me, Lord, with my disbelief. It is my deepest desire to live a confident life in You and live out loud as an example for my family and community. Help me to grow and hear Your still, small voice. Guide me in the right path to take each and every day, Amen.

Mentoring Tip: It's important to learn to balance your Christian life with Grace and Truth.

CONVERSATION 4

What Can God Do With My Regrets?

Brothers and sisters, I do not consider myself yet to have taken hold of it. But one thing I do: Forgetting what is behind and straining toward what is ahead, I press on toward the goal to win the prize for which God has called me heavenward in Christ Jesus. Philippians 3:13-15 (NIV)

Day 1: Pressing On

You know the feeling. It strikes after you buy a new pair of shoes. Or maybe after you eat a second bowl of ice cream. Or maybe after you agree to help at the school's bake sale when you had a dozen other commitments.

Regret. It hits hard, sinks deep, and holds on no matter how hard you try to let it go. It's the cold, all-consuming feeling you did something you shouldn't have done, or you didn't do something you should have. No one is immune to regret.

The Bible doesn't pull punches. God's Word will only tell truths that transform lives. Any other book would gloss over the foolish choices or rebellious behaviors of its main characters, but not the Bible. The Bible lays everything out. No polish, no faking, and no excuses.

If there's one person in the Bible with reason to cling to his regrets, it would be the Apostle Paul. Born with a different name, Saul, spent his life as a highly trained Jewish leader determined to imprison, persecute, and kill

Christians. He wasn't a nice guy, Saul. But God had bigger plans for him, and Jesus Himself confronted Saul in Acts 9. Guess what happened next?

Saul became a dynamic leader in the early church and founded the concept of world missions. He also wrote more than half of the New Testament.

Philippians is a brief but powerful letter from Paul to the Church at Philippi. The Book of Philippians emphasizes joy in troubled times and addresses how to be strong in the power of the Lord even when life doesn't go as planned. Philippians is one of those books you'd want if you were stranded on a desert island with no hope of rescue because even when you'd lost all hope, God could give you another reason to keep on hoping.

One of the hallmarks of Paul's writing style is his constant use of sports metaphors. Throughout the letters he wrote, Paul uses different sports like running, boxing, and wrestling to present a picture of what the Christian life is like.

Now you may not be into sports, but you can appreciate the idea of running a race. Maybe you're not a marathon runner, but you can acknowledge what it would feel like to cross the finish line.

Open your Bible to Philippians 3:14 and write this verse in the space below, highlighting the words you care about the most.

_____

_____

Saul, who would later become known as the Apostle Paul, wrote 13 of the 27 books in the New Testament, the second half of the Bible. Sometimes these 13 books are called the Pauline Epistles (an *epistle* is another word for a *letter*). They are as follows: Romans, 1 Corinthians, 2 Corinthians, Galatians, Ephesians, Philippians, Colossians, 1 Thessalonians, 2 Thessalonians, 1 Timothy, 2 Timothy, Titus, and Philemon.

Paul wrote these letters to people and churches, but first-century churches were a little different than the churches of today. For one, there were no denominations. A city didn't have a Baptist church and a Catholic church and a Presbyterian church; cities in the first century had temples dedicated to false gods. And the Church (capital C) didn't usually have a building. The Church was a body of people who met (sometimes in secret) to worship God.

So when Paul addressed a letter to the Church at Philippi or the Church at Ephesus or the Church in Corinth, those letters didn't go to a mailbox or an email account. They were scribbled on animal skin or parchment and delivered by hand to someone in charge of the city's one Church.

It's a little different from the multi-denominational church-mania we have going on in America today, isn't it?

Using Paul's terminology, what race are we running?

_____

What do you think is on the other side of the finish line?

_____

If the Christian life is a race, what stage would you say you're in right now? Circle one.

- I don't race.
- I've got the uniform, but I don't think it fits me.
- I'm in the locker room, gearing up.
- I'm on the sidelines.
- I'm warming up at the starting position.
- I'm ready to race.
- I'm at the halfway point, ready for a break.
- The finish line is in sight.

Where would you like to be?

_____

Think about running in a race. Which direction do you face? _____

Maybe you think it's a funny question, but when you live your life weighed down with regrets, what you're doing is running a race looking backward. Picture it. Running backwards. You collide with people and objects. You have to go slow because you aren't sure where you're heading, and you can't see what's coming next.

Living with regrets not only blinds you to both dangers and amazing opportunities around you, but it makes you less effective, less energetic, and less confident.

What regrets are draining your energy today?

_____

_____

Read 2 Timothy 4:7 (ESV).

> **"I have fought the good fight, I have finished the race, I have kept the faith."**

What is keeping you from turning loose of your regrets so you can fight the good fight and press forward to the finish line?

_____

_____

You can win. Victory is already yours in Jesus. Reach out and take it.

"You don't get rid of yesterday by talking about it all of the time; you get rid of its effect on you by moving forward." — Chrystal Evans Hurst

Select your favorite verse from Day 1 then flip forward to Day 5 of this chapter and record it in the top box. For the rest of today spend time in prayer meditating and living out the verse you selected.

A Prayer

Dear God, where do I start? Is it really possible to press on and forget what's behind me? I never want to talk about my regrets with anyone, but today I choose to talk to You. I'm finally beginning to learn You are real, present, and listening to me. Help me to trust You with my painful, secret regrets. It's easier to give grace to other people than it is to show grace to myself. Am I stuck on being right and doing right? Have I forgotten to allow You into those dark places in my life? I choose to surrender my heart and wait on You to move in a powerful way. You created time and never waste one minute of it, so help me to grow in my faith and trust You with my past regrets. I want to start living again but this time without my regrets. I'm leaving all the pain and regrets at the foot of the cross. Have Your way, oh Lord. In Your victorious name I pray, Amen.

Day 2: Not "Who" but "Whose" I am
Elisabeth Elliot: One Day At A Time

When I was in my early 30s, my mentor invited me to an event where Elisabeth Elliot was the keynote speaker. I'd never heard of her before, but time away with my mentor sounded like fun regardless of what we were doing. So off to Lancaster, PA we drove, and as I sat in the church listening to Elisabeth Elliot speak, I could sense immediately how intentional she was about her faith and prayer life. She had a soft, deep, genuine voice, and I knew this Christian woman, missionary, speaker, and author was someone God had sent my way to guide and encourage me in my walk with Him.

Elisabeth Elliot told us about her radio show, *Gateway to Joy*. She told us, "Everything, if given to God, can become your gateway to joy." I started listening to her radio show, and she opened every segment with the following statement:

> **"You are loved with an everlasting love, and underneath are the everlasting arms."**

Elisabeth Elliot is one of the most influential Christian women of our time. She is the widow of Jim Elliot, who was martyred for his faith deep in the jungles of Ecuador on January 8, 1956. Before she was 30, she was a widow, and not through disease or accidental death—murder of the most brutal and vicious kind all because her husband loved Jesus and wanted to tell people about Him.[13]

But Elisabeth Elliot wasn't just a daughter, wife, mother, widow, and missionary; she was a Jesus-follower. She knew "whose" she was; she belonged to God. She put one foot in front of the other. She took one day at a time and did what needed to be done right then, without focusing on what could have been or what should have been.

The result? Through her life and her testimony, through her bravery in sharing her experiences, she brought the message of Christ to men and women around the world.

What regret from your past could become your gateway to joy today?

What is keeping you from giving your regrets to God?

_____

Look up the following verses and write down the word they all have in common in the space provided:

- Psalm 37:23
- Proverbs 16:9
- Job 31:4

What word do all these verses have in common? _____

Are you encouraged? Conversation 1, Day 1, we read Malachi 3:16-17. This amazing passage told us God listens to our conversations. Now, we learn God also orders our every step when we lean on Him and trust Him.

> Here's a perfect moment to lay down your pen and say a prayer of thanksgiving to your Heavenly Father for His love and care for you.

Our worlds are busy, and they're getting busier every day. Each moment, some new distraction is vying for your attention, so you need to be careful. You need to guard your heart. Are you reading good, godly material and listening to godly speakers for Christ who encourage you and inspire you on a daily basis? Be alert and selective when you are choosing who you listen to, where you go, and who influences you, because those choices will determine who you become.

When we are overwhelmed by life and its responsibilities, when our friends and family and relationships need our attention, when our careers and personal health require our focus, it's easy to drown in the rising tide of the urgent. But something urgent doesn't automatically become something important. It's easy to look forward and plan or dream, but the more you focus on the future, the less power you have for right now.

Sometimes all you need to do is take the next step.

"When you don't know what to do next, just do the thing in front of you." - Elisabeth Elliot

Now let's dig into a person in the Bible who was willing to take the next step that was right in front of her.

Mary of Bethany: She Did What She Could

Earlier this week, we talked about the Apostle Paul and the massive role he played in the writing and distribution of the Gospel throughout the world, but the Bible doesn't only talk about big names. The Bible isn't all about major conversion stories and dramatic plot twists. Sometimes the Bible tells us about someone who wasn't important at all in the grand scheme of history. This is how we meet Mary of Bethany.

> Mary joins the other Marys we read about in Scripture. She's mentioned several times. She's one of Jesus' friends and disciples, and she's a traditional Jewish woman from the first century. But Mary of Bethany has a claim to fame. What she did sets her apart from the others, and her simple action has been and will continue to be memorialized for thousands of years.[14]

Turn in your Bible to Mark 14:3-9 and read this incredible story. What was happening in this house?

_____

What did Mary break?

_____

What was inside? What did she do with it?

_____

Such an extravagant display of love and affection toward Jesus could only be admired, right? Or was it? What did Jesus' disciples have to say about it?

_____

Write down Jesus' response from verse 6 in these three spaces:

_____

_____

_____

I am so encouraged by Jesus' response to Mary's actions in Mark 14. From this one scripture, we are reminded God sees every beautiful thing we do for him and for others.

What is the most touching, most memorable act you've ever seen one person do for another?

_____

_____

If we are followers of Christ, we are to have a beautiful scent others recognize in multiple ways. Write out 2 Corinthians 2:14 below.

_____

_____

How can you spread this Christ-like aroma for your family? At work? In your church?

_____

_____

What Mary of Bethany did for Jesus in this moment was bigger than anyone knew. People didn't realize it, but Jesus was going to His death. Only a couple of verses later, Jesus would be betrayed, arrested, condemned, and brutally killed. Some people have theorized while Jesus hung on the cross, He would still have been able to smell the sweet aroma of Mary's extravagant perfume.

What Mary did for Him with what she had was good. If she'd had something else to give Him, she might have done something different. **The point isn't what she did; the point is why.**

Mary acted where she was with what she had, purposefully and intentionally seeking to bless Jesus, to do something kind for Him. Now, everywhere the Gospel is preached, people remember her and what she did.

For some of us, maybe our past hasn't always presented a Christ-like attitude of the Gospel. When you look back on your life, you have two options. You can regret what you've done, where you've come from, or the choices you've made, or you can learn from them, recognize God is bigger than your failures, and press forward for Him.

Maybe you're like Elisabeth Elliot, and your life hasn't turned out like you planned. You've experience unimaginable heartbreak. And all you can think about is how your life might have been less painful if you'd walked down a different path.

Maybe you're like Mary of Bethany, and you've done something bold and extravagant for Jesus. But instead of accolades and praise and support, you've heard nothing but criticism or negativity. And you don't understand, because you're doing all this for God. So why don't other God-followers have your back? You're starting to think you made a mistake or maybe you wasted so much time in your past.

In the end, those feelings of regret are guilt in disguise.

Today is a new day. Let's grow closer to our Savior Jesus Christ and move from the outer sidelines to a place of authenticity and live our lives being held closely in the arms of God.

Say this truth out loud to yourself on a daily basis: "God doesn't waste time or discouragement. Nothing is wasted. It's all for God's glory."

"Don't allow the weight of discouragement to hold you down or lower your expectations of the abundant life in Christ." – Sharon Jaynes

We mentioned in Day 1 how highly educated Paul was. His parents may have done everything they could to provide the best education for him so he could become a high-ranking Jewish leader. They must have been disappointed in him when he committed his life to Christ. They may have thought his life was a waste when he became a leader for the Way. But God had a plan and a purpose for Paul's life. God used every moment of Paul's education and past training to further His Kingdom and bring glory to His name.

Guess what? At this very moment, God is working out His plan for you and for me too.

Read Romans 8:28 (NASB). **"And we know that God causes all**

things to work together for good to those who love God, to those who are called according to His purpose."

Be encouraged. No regrets. **Nothing is wasted. It's all for God's glory.**

Write out three specific actions you can take today to start living without regrets:

1. _____

2. _____

3. _____

Select your favorite verse from Day 2 then flip forward to Day 5 of this chapter and record it in the top box. For the rest of today spend time in prayer meditating and living out the verse you selected.

A Prayer

Oh Lord Jesus, please help me know how much I mean to You. I long to hear Your voice and know Your love in a deep, rich way. I'm really struggling with all my responsibilities. I'm overwhelmed. I know You are able and willing to rescue me. Please, Lord. Won't You rescue me? I humbly come before You with my heart and hands wide open. Do whatever it takes to make me into the person You created me to be for Your Glory. Holy Spirit, show me how to live the victorious life in You one day at a time. I will trust You. I believe You are by my side. You're my Healer and all I need. In the matchless, incredibly powerful name of Jesus Christ I pray, Amen.

Day 3: With Me, It's All or Nothing

"With me, it's all or nothing!" If you're like me and you come from a theater background, you probably sang those words out loud with a bit of a southern twang. For the rest of you, it's all right. We're probably a little crazy. It's the title of one of the songs from the famous Rodgers and Hammerstein musical *Oklahoma*, and if you're familiar with it at all, you can't help but sing along.

In this song, character Will Parker addresses flirtatious Ado Annie about the rumors he's heard about her behavior. He demands if she wants to be in a relationship with him—well, with him, it's all or nothing.

Some of us take an all-or-nothing stance with our task lists, right? Or our goals for the future? We determine to accomplish everything on our list, and if we don't, we're failures.

Today, God is calling us to put Jesus in the center of everything we do, not only in the parts of our life where He's convenient.

It's good and acceptable to only give God a few hours a week at church in volunteering to help others. But giving God everything, using our time and skills and passion to mentor the next generation is totally off the church's radar screen. I believe each of us can change lives one heartbeat at a time, starting with our hearts.

You may be thinking, "Jayme, really? Do we need to give God everything?"

Let's dig into Revelation 3:16

"So because you are lukewarm, neither hot nor cold, I am about to spit you out of my mouth. I wish you were either one or the other."

God is clear about where he wants you and me to stand, but in order to be all in with Jesus, we need to be willing to give Him our worries, disappointments, past failures, and pain.

In the book *How to Walk in the Supernatural Power of God*, Guillermo Maldonoado says, **"The only ability God requires is availability."**

It is my deepest desire for us to let go of our past, all those regrets holding us captive, and tell God we will give Him our everything. We need to be all in with Jesus.

Let's decide: With us, it's all or nothing.

> Take a second and talk to God about your schedule. Ask Him to show you where you're too focused on what doesn't matter.

God's Word	Write God's Promise	Prayer Time
John 15:14-15		Pray and thank God for being your friend
Psalm 25:9		Pray and thank God He blesses the humble
James 4:6		Pray and thank God He gives us grace

Select your favorite verse from Day 3 then flip forward to Day 5 of this chapter and record it in the top box. For the rest of today spend time in prayer meditating and living out the verse you selected.

A Prayer

Oh Holy Spirit, show me the way to go from here. I'm learning so much about Your love for me. I want to live a life full of Your peace and joy more and more every day. Thank You for not giving up on me or leaving me. Even though I'm impatient with myself, I realize You are incredibly patient with me. Thank You for holding me in Your arms and loving me over and over again. I'm fighting my discouragement and despair through Your Scriptures. Most of all, I'm praying for Your guidance and hope. I want to be completely ALL IN. Thank You for working all things together for my good and Your glory, Amen.

Day 4: Know Where To Take Your Questions

I can waste so much time and brain space trying to rearrange and squeeze everything into my schedule for the day or week. I continuously talk about how I need to change this, but my busyness rears its ugly head and peeks in through the cracks wherever it can. Can you relate?

Every time I begin to falter in my commitments to read Scripture and fellowship with other believers, my life starts falling apart. If I don't reach out to my mentor for encouragement, inspiration, and accountability it shows in my attitude and my approach to life. I've learned the busier I become, the more time I need to spend with God in prayer as well as in conversations with my mentor.

Look up each verse and begin plugging in your matches.

Psalm 5:11	_____	Submit to God and draw near to Him
Psalm 121:1-2	_____	God calls us His friends
Amos 3:7	_____	Joy promised for those who take refuge in God
John 15:15	_____	God reveals His plans to those who hear His Word
James 4:7-8	_____	Our help comes from the Lord

Regardless of whether you work outside or inside the home, you're busy. One of the oldest tricks in the enemy's playbook is to make us so busy we forget what really matters. So how do you handle it?

Much like guilt, the feeling of regret doesn't make you better. It's a paralytic. Your regrets keep you focused on the past and everything you did wrong. Instead, God calls you to look toward the future. His Grace sets you free from the demons in your past and the would-have, could-have, should-haves holding you back. Don't let anyone or any regret destroy your shining light for Jesus.

Here are four key strategies to cope with busyness and live a life without regret.

1. Get your rest

"If we do not practice the habit of a restful life, we will end up with serious illness, exhaustion, bad attitudes, and fist-shaking faith aimed heavenly." - Sally Clarkson

75

The more exhausted I get, the grumpier I become, and before you know it, there is no more joy. Learning to rest is a choice. Learning to give rest to your heart, mind, and soul is a blessing from heaven.

Write Mark 6:31 as a reminder of what the Lord longs for us to do in seeking rest.

_____

_____

2. Ask for help from others

"We're all imperfect, and we all have needs. The weak usually do not ask for help, so they stay weak. If we recognize that we are imperfect, we will ask for help, and we will pray for the guidance necessary to bring positive results to whatever we are doing."
- John Wooden

Are you willing to ask for help? People in our world think asking for help is a sign of weakness, or they see it as a forerunner to failure. Not true. Here are four facts to remember about asking for help:

- Asking for help is the hallmark of great leaders
- Asking for help doesn't make you a burden or someone who is out of control
- Asking for help gives another person the chance to use their gifts and talents to do what they do best
- Asking for help demonstrates your character as a person, stating you aren't perfect, you're humble, and you're teachable.

Write Matthew 7:7 on the line below:

_____

*On the chart below, write down what you need to
ask, seek, or find today in prayer with God.*
My Heart Needs To:

ASK	SEEK	KNOCK

3. Simplify
**"If you entrust God with your 'here,' He will take you
'there.'" Christine Caine**

Simplifying is freeing, but getting there and making the decision to simplify can be overwhelming. Nevertheless, if we want to live without regrets, we must simplify our lives.

Nancy DeMoss Wolgemuth created a wonderful resource to help us keep the first things first. She uses an acronym for the word *priorities*. It's listed below. Underline the ones you need the most today.

- **P**ray
- **R**eview and receive God's priorities for your life
- **I**nventory
- **O**rder your schedule and activities
- **R**esist the tyranny of the urgent
- **I**nput from other people
- **T**ake advantage of the time God gives you
- **I**dentify time robbers
- **E**xperience this season and this moment fully
- **S**abbath rest with sensitivity and surrender to the Spirit

4. Seek a mentor

First, pay attention to the people in your circle. Watch the people who are already in your life. Maybe a neighbor you walk with has caught your eye. Possibly you noticed someone who volunteers with you at the local rescue mission.

Second, be courageous. Walk across the room and say hello. Start the conversation.

Third, tell this person how you've watched them and admire them. Ask if the two of you could meet for coffee or go for a walk sometime.

Fourth, follow through. Be on time. Don't cancel. Pray before you get together and ask God to create a new mentoring relationship with this godly, mature Christian.

Fifth, be gracious. Listen. Say thank you. Tell them how blessed you are to have conversations about real-life issues and God. Ask if you could get together again sometime.

Select your favorite verse from Day 4 then flip forward to Day 5 of this chapter and record it in the top box. For the rest of today spend time in prayer meditating and living out the verse you selected.

A Prayer

Heavenly Father, I praise You for Your amazing love. Thank You for the tender nudge to my soul to live a more simplified life with You by my side. I can't do life alone. I need You. I need others. I'm listening, God. Please speak to me and tell me the direction to take. Show me how to let go of the hinderances in my life and hold on to what keeps the flame burning for You. I've been so foolish in the past, and I'm hesitant to step out and totally trust You. Forgive me. Help me learn how to walk away from my past hurts, failures, pain, and disappointments once and for all. With You by my side, I believe all things are possible. All of this I ask in the precious name of Jesus, Amen.

"If I seldom talk with God, it indicates He plays a secondary role in my life. Soon the world demands more attention than does God." - E.M. Bounds

Day 5: Prayer Plan for the Finish Line

As you complete each daily section of this study, write down your favorite verse from each day.

Day 1: _____

Day 2: _____

Day 3: _____

Day 4: _____

The Greeks had a special relay race in the Olympic games called a *lampadedromia*, where runners carried torches throughout the race. But this race wasn't about finishing. The winner wasn't the first person to cross over the finish line. It was the first person to cross the finish line with their torch still lit.

It's one thing to finish a race. It's something else to finish well.

Starting a race and pressing on toward the finish line is so important, but God also cares about how we finish. Be encouraged. You can do this. You can live a life without regrets.

"Faith is like lighting the torch that passes from one person to the next. You can't light the torch of another if yours isn't burning." – Charles Swindoll

We are all running the race of the Christian life, but the truth is, we've already won. You've already got a medal around your neck, and Jesus already put His trophy on your shelf. Our names are engraved in the Lamb's Book of Life, and nothing can ever erase them.

There are obstacles in our paths to overcome. There are people in our lives we are designed to help. God has given us goals and dreams He wants to help us achieve. We still have a race to run. But you don't have to run alone.

> Close your eyes. Put down your pen or pencil. The Lord cares about how you finish your race. Tell Him what His care means to you.

Journaling the Journey

1. How will you take what you've learned this week and apply it to your life today?

_____

_____

_____

2. What are two or three ways you can live without regret and fan the flame of Christ in your heart?

_____

_____

_____

3. What person(s) inspires you to live without regrets and press on toward Christ? What draws you to them and their story?

_____

_____

_____

A Prayer

I praise You, Lord and Creator of my soul. I quietly wait on You for my guidance and direction. I confess I have a hard time surrendering to Your will. Please forgive me. I know I can't do this life alone; I need You. Today I choose to believe and trust You with my entire life. Help me to be alert and watching for Your hand in my life. I know I'm blessed when I follow where You lead me. Please Lord, protect me. Help me to desire to know You in my heart more and more each day. Right now, I thank You for the change in my life as I draw closer to You day by day. In the holy name of Jesus I pray, Amen.

Mentoring Tip: A Mentor reminds you that nothing is wasted. God will use your heartache and suffering for good.

A Note From Jayme:

Hey there friends. Congratulations! You are half way through the study and meeting with God on a daily basis. Don't give up. God has something special in store for you in the second half of the study. Be encouraged! You, the Holy Spirit and your mentor can do this! Blessings!

Where Is God When I'm Exhausted?

Jesus said, "Come off by yourselves; let's take a break and get a little rest." For there was constant coming and going. They didn't even have time to eat. Mark 6:31 (MSG)

Day 1: Forethought or Afterthought?

Vacation is a time when you leave behind the stress and responsibility of your everyday life and have fun, refreshing adventures with your loved ones. Camping in the mountains. Fishing on a lake. Seeing the sights. Indulging in local cuisine. Walking along the beach at sunset.

But if you have ever planned a vacation where you tried to cram in as much activity as possible, you know that vacations often come with stress too. You've got a limited amount of time, so you want to get the most bang for your buck. You don't want to miss an opportunity to do something you may never get to do again.

So you load down your agenda with all sorts of things to do and see, and before long, you're wishing you were back home so you could rest. By the end, you need a vacation from your vacation!

Then, it hits you: *Did I ask God about my vacation agenda?*

No wonder I'm a mess. No wonder I can't balance my time.

Can you recall a time in your life when you went forward with a plan, agenda, vacation, job, or project without consulting God about it? Describe your situation.

_____

_____

I never knew God was interested in every detail of my scheduled life until I read Psalm 37:23. Highlight or circle the keywords that start with the letter D.

> *The Lord directs the steps of the godly. He*
> *delights in every detail of their lives.*

Jesus is our role model and sets the example for our lives, whether it is work or rest. Notice in Mark 6:31, our key verse for today, that Jesus gives us three instructions to follow:

1. Come off by yourself
2. Take a break
3. Get a little rest

Okay. Now, be gut-level honest here. Where are you in life right now? On a scale of 1 to 5, how willing are you to do the following (1 being the least willing to 5 being absolutely willing):

Willing to pause with God and get away	1	2	3	4	5
Willing to take a break	1	2	3	4	5
Willing to get a little rest	1	2	3	4	5

Circle the words that most closely describe how you feel when you are sitting still and willing to rest:

Wise   Lazy   Unproductive   Obedient   Useless   Irresponsible

Read the Psalm below:

Psalm 23

The Lord is my shepherd; I have all that I need.
He <u>lets me rest</u> in green meadows; he <u>leads</u>
<u>me</u> beside peaceful streams.
He <u>renews</u> my strength. He <u>guides</u> me along
right paths, bringing honor to his name.
Even when I walk through the darkest valley, I will
not be afraid, for you are <u>close beside me</u>. Your
rod and your staff <u>protect</u> and <u>comfort</u> me.
You <u>prepare</u> a feast for me in the presence of my
enemies. You <u>honor me</u> by anointing my head
with oil. My cup overflows with blessings.
Surely your goodness and unfailing love will pursue me all the
days of my life, and <u>I will live</u> in the house of the Lord forever.

Write the underlined words or phrases in the space provided:

1. _____   6. _____
2. _____   7. _____
3. _____   8. _____
4. _____   9. _____
5. _____   10. _____

Compare those 10 words and phrases with how you feel about resting from the words you circled first. Looking at all three charts, how does what you think and feel about your time, plans, and schedule match up with God's promises? _____

What needs to change?

_____

The Bible never tells us we should feel guilty for resting. It's the exact opposite.

Jesus rested. The Bible tells us many times that Jesus had to get away from the crowds that were constantly demanding His attention, and if Jesus can do it, so can we. Jesus recognized that He wouldn't be much good to anyone if He was too tired to do His job. That meant sometimes He had to say no to people.

"I do not want to live my life as an afterthought filled with regret. I want to be a product of forethought and rightness." - Dusty Rayburn

We are not God's afterthought.
Read Ephesians 1:4.
"God chose us to be in a relationship with Him even before He laid out plans for this world."
Likewise, if we are determined that God will not be an afterthought in our lives, everything we do on a daily basis and in our plans for the future, we will be blessed.

> Take a moment and say a prayer to God right now. Ask Him to help you identify what decisions or plans you need to talk to Him about.

Breaking the Cycle

What if the person who's asking for your time is your mom? What if it's your child? What if it's your pastor or your employer?

Setting up boundaries in our lives is one of the most divisive topics among Christians. It's easy to talk about, but in actual practice, it's far more difficult to do.

Life without boundaries may sound appealing. After all, who likes to be told no? But many times the "no's" of life keep us from getting into trouble. If we ignore them and do what we want, we usually end up putting ourselves into a corner.

A great example of what happens without boundaries is the book of Judges, a collection of stories that spans many generations within the nation of Israel.

> Judges takes place during a time before Israel had a king. During this time, Israel got caught in a vicious cycle of disobedience, and the only way God could get their attention was to allow invaders to conquer them. Repeatedly. Then, when life was so difficult that they couldn't stand it and they had no other choice, they called out to God for help. And God, as always, answered, choosing a man or a woman from among the people Israel to act as His representative to rescue the people from bondage. These specially chosen men and women were called Judges.

Some Judges may be familiar to you, such as Samson, the man with super-human strength who fell in love with the Philistine woman Delilah. Other Judges may not be familiar to you at all, like Shamgar who is only mentioned in one verse (Judges 3:31). But they all served the same purpose: They led the way back to God after the people of Israel remembered that they couldn't do life on their own terms.

Joshua, the man who succeeded Moses as the leader of Israel, died at the ripe old age of 110. He had strong words for his people, telling them that they needed to remember what God had done for them. And for a while, Israel did just that, but it didn't last forever.

Look up Judges 2:10 and fill in the empty space below:
After that generation died, another generation grew up who did not

_____

_____

_____

This is where it started. The people of Israel wanted to live the way that made them feel good. They wanted to do their own thing, regardless of what God had said was right or wrong. They wanted to make their own choices, no matter how many boundaries God had set to keep them safe.

So God let them.

Read Judges 2:18-19.

When the judge for that generation died, what did the people of Israel go after?

_____

_____

What did the people of Israel refuse to give up and let go of?

_____

_____

This vicious, damaging cycle would repeat itself at least 12 times throughout the book of Judges.

What are you holding onto with a tight grip that you know God needs you to let go of to create a more balanced life?

_____

_____

Establishing boundaries by choice

Here's our problem. For most people, we aren't trapped between a wrong choice and a right choice. Our options aren't bad versus good. Many times, we have multiple good options that God says are noble and worth doing. When our options are good, what do we do?

When your only choices honor God, and you can only choose one, how can you choose at all?

Maybe for you both job offers include potential promotions, benefits, and decent hours.

Which one should you choose?

Most of the time, we don't know so we don't choose at all. We try to do both or neglect the choice that involves putting ourselves first.

Not making a choice is the quickest path to a meltdown, and all of us have been on that road. Some of us are there today.

But we don't have to be there any longer.

God never motivates through guilty feelings. Never. He is not a manipulator. And He has never asked us to perform to a standard so that we could deserve His love. That's the exact opposite of His Word.

Speak the following declaration out loud to yourself today:

"I am not alone. God is by my side. I can do this!"

Now say it again like you really mean it. Look at yourself in the mirror and say it. Stand up and shout it at the rooftops. Write it on an index card and carry it with you.

Check out Psalm 118:6 (NLT).

> **The Lord is for me, so I will have no fear. What can mere people do to me?**

Explain the following phrases from Psalm 118:6 in your own words:

"The Lord is for me":

_____

"What can mere people do":

_____

God is all about relationships, balance, and boundaries, whether they are boundaries between right and wrong or if they are boundaries between good and best. He created them, and He wants us to integrate them into our lives in a healthy and productive way. If you want to find balance for your life and your family, it starts with setting godly boundaries, and the first step to godly boundaries is to ask God for help identifying them.

Look up James 1:5.

If you need wisdom, what should you do?

_____

What will God do?

_____

What will God NOT do?

_____

"Don't ever hesitate to tell [God] whatever is on your heart. He already knows it anyway, but He doesn't want you to bear its pain or celebrate its joy alone." - Billy Graham

Select your favorite verse from Day 1 then flip forward to Day 5 of this chapter and record it in the top box. For the rest of today spend time in prayer meditating and living out the verse you selected.

A Prayer

Oh Jesus, I need You. I tell everyone You are my best friend, but do I really treat You that way? I'm sorry. I know I haven't been a good best friend in return. The world is crazy, and so is my schedule. Help me regroup. I want to choose to live my life the way You would want me to, but I'm so exhausted. I've ignored Your warning signs, and my boundaries are wimpy, help me recover and be strong. You say in Ephesians 6:10 (MSG), *"God is strong, and he wants you strong. So take everything the Master has set out for You, well-made weapons of the best materials. And put them to use so You will be able to stand up to everything the devil throws Your way."* Today I choose You. Guide me with every step I take. Thank goodness You are a patient God. Let's go. It's You and me God, together. In Your Holy name I pray. Amen!

Day 2: Boundaries Are a God Thing

When someone you don't want to talk to calls you on your cell phone, what do you do? You use the "block caller" feature, right? Cell phones make this easy. One click, and you never have to be bothered by that person again.

No awkward explanations. No uncomfortable confrontations. It's wonderful.

But there isn't a "block caller" feature for face-to-face conversations. We have to deal with people at work, at church, at the supermarket, or in other places in our daily lives, and without boundaries and balance, life and its never-ending "one more thing" will overwhelm us.

There's always one more item on the to-do list. There's always one more meeting to attend. There's always one more email to send, one more task to complete, one more phone call to make. And if you can't get everything done, you see yourself as a failure or that you don't measure up.

In our culture of financial stability and material success, we've cultivated a lifestyle of performance standards that are impossible to sustain. If we're being honest, none of us are capable of consistently achieving those impossible standards. And if we're being really honest, most people don't even expect it.

What would happen if you and I forge a new perspective on boundaries? Let's rethink. We are always a work in progress. Life with God is a journey. The Holy Spirit stands ready to guide us through our day, helping us set boundaries and find a healthy balance. Living that way is refreshing and renews our mind in a biblical, spiritual sense.

Our culture-wide perspective on productivity and achievement won't allow us to rest; we fill our hours with activities so that we haven't wasted our time. But there's a vast difference between wasting your time and resting.

This is where God's concept of boundaries come into the equation. Yes, the idea of creating boundaries in life started with God in Genesis 1:1-23. Not because God needed to rest, but so that we would have an example of how to live.

Look up Hebrews 4:9-11.
Why are we to rest from our works?

_____

What effort are we supposed to make in order to enter that rest?

_____

The Bible has a lot to say about boundaries and balance in our lives, and it's time we, as Christians in a world that's busier than ever, take a moment to see what God really expects from us.

Look up Psalm 16:6 and fill in the blanks:
    The boundary lines have fallen for me in _____ places; surely I have a _____ inheritance.
    Would you have ever associated those two words with the concept of boundaries?

    Usually when we think about setting boundaries, we focus on saying no or turning people down or disappointing our loved ones. If we look at it that way, how could saying no ever result in a happy outcome?

When was the last time you told someone no?

_____

When was the last time you told someone yes, even though you should have said no?

_____

What happened as a result?

_____

Fill in the blanks with the time you spend daily on each activity:

	_____ hrs Sleep
	_____ hrs Work/Commute
	_____ hrs Cooking
	_____ hrs Family time
	_____ hrs Housework
	_____ hrs Help with Homework
	_____ hrs School activities
	_____ hrs Shopping
	_____ hrs Time with friends
	_____ hrs Quiet Time with Jesus
	_____ hrs On Digital Devices
	_____ hrs Personal care time
	_____ hrs Church activities

Add those numbers up and put the total here: _____

If that number is more than 24, you must be a time traveler.

Nobody gets more than 24 hours in a day. We're all subject to the same laws of time, and trying to do too much is not only destroying our lives, it's hurting our relationships. So let's get one thing straight: **The idea that we have to run ourselves ragged in the name of Jesus doesn't come from God.** And if it doesn't come from God, there's only one other place it could come from: the enemy.

> Take a moment and say a prayer to God right now. Ask Him to help you identify the things in your life that really matter.

Look up the following verses and summarize them on the lines provided:
Psalm 127:2

_____

_____

Proverbs 16:25

_____

_____

Matthew 11:28-30

_____

_____

Philippians 4:6-7

_____

_____

God created boundaries

Starting in the Book of Genesis, at the very beginning, God created boundaries between light and darkness, the land and the sky, the animals and man. Creation itself is a reflection of what healthy boundaries should look like, and just like in the Garden of Eden, the enemy is all about telling us that boundaries don't matter.

He's a liar. And ignoring healthy boundaries in our lives will be devastating to us, just as it was to Adam and Eve.

We attribute about half of the Psalms to King David. You want to talk about someone who learned a thing or two about healthy boundaries? David's your man.

David is largely regarded as the greatest king of Israel, but more than that, God calls David a man after His own heart.

A Closer Look at The Psalms

- Psalms has the most chapters in the Bible (150 of them)
- The Psalms were written over a period of 1,000 years
- Psalm 22 vividly describes crucifixion before it was invented
- Psalm 90 is believed one of the oldest chapters in the Bible, written by Moses
- Psalms is divided into five sections, with each section corresponding to one of the first five books of the Bible. Each one ends with a doxology of sorts.
  - o Psalms 1-41 (Genesis)
  - o Psalms 42-72 (Exodus)
  - o Psalms 73-89 (Leviticus)
  - o Psalms 90-106 (Numbers)
  - o Psalms 107-150 (Deuteronomy)

Would you like God to say that about you?

I would.

But what's interesting to note is that while David was a successful and renowned king, his personal life was a mess. He made some really awful choices concerning his family, and most of his children went off the rails.

So much of the trauma that David's family experienced could have been avoided if he'd simply kept some godly boundaries in his life.

So what kind of boundaries was David missing? Where do we even start?

- He didn't set boundaries on his marriages (he had more than one wife).
- He didn't set boundaries on his parenting (his kids were beyond troubled).

He didn't set boundaries on his job (he made some foolish choices as king too).

Since he didn't know when to say no, David lost track of what mattered. By the end of this life, he'd committed adultery and murder, and his own children wanted him dead.

Yes, this is the same David we're talking about. This is the Man after God's Own Heart. This man wrote half of the longest book in the Bible. This man is recognized as one of the greatest God-followers in history.

How could God use someone who had messed up so completely?

Dear friends, that's what our great God does.

God doesn't pull His punches with Scripture. The Bible lays out all the failures and sins of great men like David for us to read for ourselves. We know every wrong move David made, and we also know how God redeemed David's failures to do miracles.

That's just who God is, and He's the same today as He was when David wrote the Psalms.

What words of encouragement can you write in the following space to yourself?

_____

_____

Now, imagine God actually saying those encouraging words to you, directly into your heart right now. Because that's what He sees.

If you were willing accept that God loves you and has your best future in mind, how would that change the way you live?

_____

_____

God has amazing plans for you. He wants to take you on the greatest adventure of a lifetime, and He's just waiting for you to say yes to Him. But you've got to turn over the guilt you still feel, and then, you've got to build some boundaries into your life to prevent you from going down that old road of exhaustion again.

Select your favorite verse from Day 2 then flip forward to Day 5 of this chapter and record it in the top box. For the rest of today spend time in prayer meditating and living out the verse you selected.

A Prayer

Holy Spirit, I'm in a really bad spot right now. I can't even put words to my feelings. I'm trying. Please just listen to my heart. I'm so alone, distracted, and overloaded that I sometimes forget to call out to You. Speak to me today. Right now, I give You complete permission to change my life. I want to follow You with all my heart. I believe You have a better plan for me than what I had for myself. It seems like I keep going ahead with my own plans and end up wounded. Move me to where You want me. Help me lay down my failures and pick up the boundaries You set for me. I need Your grace to balance out my life. I need You Jesus. I'm totally out of control, and I need You to move forward. Forgive me. Heal me. Move me. Speak to me, Holy Spirit. Amen

Day 3: Bold Humility, Quiet Strength
Janet Parshall: Planning Boundaries God's Way

I find myself constantly thinking: I wish I had more time. If not that, I wonder where all my time has disappeared to. What about you?

We are weighed down with so many commitments and responsibilities that we have no down time. Some people call it *free time*. Now that's a funny thought. What is free time? When has time ever been free?

Have you ever agreed with someone out loud just because it was easier than sharing how you really felt? And besides that, who has time to really discuss how they feel anyway? Maybe it was a coworker, boss, or teacher. Maybe it was a friend or someone you admired. Or maybe it was the topic itself that made you uncomfortable—politics, religion, sex, or Jesus Himself.

When it comes to tough conversations, the path of least resistance is certainly easier to walk, and you won't rock the boat as much. But what if rocking the boat is part of our responsibilities? God specifically gives us a permission slip to make time to communicate about anything with anyone at any time for His glory.

> **"You will never find time for anything. If you want time, you must make it." – Charles Bixton**

I believe without boundaries and balance in our lives, we can easily be led astray. That's why it's crucial to have godly influences in our lives and a mentor you can spend time with on a regular basis.

One of my godly influencers I turn to for advice and insight is Janet Parshall. Janet is a noted Christian radio host of the In The Market Podcast on Moody Radio. She has to make the choice to have tough conversations every day as part of her career.[15]

Janet began her career in radio many years ago but has never backed away from standing up for her faith in Jesus Christ, regardless of who she interviewed or what topics were raised on her shows. Her shows are broadcast to more than 80 radio stations where she discusses issues that affect the family, such as homosexuality, pornography, abortion, civil rights and more.[16]

Have you ever had to challenge someone else's statements because they weren't biblically sound? _____
Recall the situation.

_____

_____

_____

Do you believe your own boundaries are more important or less important than someone else's? _____
Explain your answer.

_____

_____

_____

Janet's passion is to equip God's people through intelligent conversation based on the Word of God. She isn't afraid to discuss the challenging major news stories and relevant issues being debated in the marketplace, and she speaks with bold humility to those around her with the Truth of God's Word.

What relevant issues are at the top of your list for discussions today? List four current events or news stories tugging on your heart that you would love to discuss:

1. _____
2. _____
3. _____
4. _____

Review your list and circle the one subject you'd like to hear discussed on Janet's show or in your conversation with your mentor.

America today is more confused than it has ever been, and women like Janet Parshall are taking steps to rebuild the boundaries that have crumbled under the weight of political correctness.

But not all of us run a podcast, right? Very few of us even have enough connections in our lives to influence anyone who matters. So what difference can we make?

Setting godly boundaries and sticking to them will change the way people around you think about you and your faith. Many Christian women ask me during our mentoring relationship sessions how to stand boldly in their faith.

Let's look at one of the most encouraging verses in the Bible, Hebrews 4:16. This verse will encourage us to create a plan that helps us learn to set boundaries and find balance in our daily lives.

Write Hebrews 4:16 below:

_____

_____

Be encouraged as we dig into this wonderful verse. What I love about this verse is how God issues an open invitation to us to come before His throne and talk to Him.

Keyword Study & Simple Steps
Hebrews 4:16 (NIV)
Part 1: "Let us then **approach** the throne
of **grace** with **confidence**."

#1: Approach
1. Write Webster's definition for the word *approach*:

_____

2. Prayer is how we approach the throne of grace.
3. Open Invitation. As a child of God and follower of Christ, we have been given an open invitation to approach God's throne of grace.

#2: Grace
1. When you hear the word *grace*, what thoughts come to mind?

_____

_____

2. Scripture tells followers of Christ that grace is receiving a gift from God that we don't deserve. Grace cannot be earned and we don't deserve it but God freely gives us His gift of grace. No matter what our sin, God's amazing grace is still available to those who believe in Him.

3. God's grace reveals His unfailing love that is unending and unlimited.

Take a moment and spend some time in prayer, thanking God for His gift of grace in your life.

**"Between here and heaven, every minute that the Christian lives will be a minute of grace."
– Charles Hadden Spurgeon**

#3: Confidence

1. Write Webster's definition of the word *confidence*:

_____

2. Confidence comes as we practice our approach (defined in #1) on a daily basis. Every action step to approach the throne of grace builds our confidence.

3. Scripture is truth. We stand with confidence according to Scripture. Part 2: "So that we may **receive mercy** and **find grace** in our time of need."

#4: Receive Mercy

1. Mercy can be defined as follows: *Not being punished for an offense you committed.*

2. The Greek word that is translated as *receive* in Hebrews 4:16 means to *actively accept.*

3. Combine those two concepts in your mind and write out what that idea means to you personally:

_____

#5: Find Grace

1. Write Webster's definition of the verb *find*:

_____

2. Grace isn't something that we are able to achieve in our own strength. It's not something we have to struggle to attain. It's a free gift that God has already extended to us, in spite of the fact that we can't ever earn it.
3. Explain the difference between grace and mercy in your own words.

"God doesn't just give us grace; He gives us Jesus, the Lord of grace." Joni Eareckson Tada

Write down the names of three people you have direct influence over, whether in your family, your career, or your personal relationships.

1. _____
2. _____
3. _____

You have more influence than you know. More people look up to you or admire you than you realize. Someone is always watching, whether you realize it or not. That's why it's so important to know where you stand, why you stand, and then stand there.

Look up Matthew 5:37.
What is your "Yes" supposed to mean?

_____

What is your "No" supposed to mean?

_____

What do you think your relationships would look if you lived by this rule?

_____

It's important to note, though, that Janet Parshall didn't ascend to her position in the political arena by bulldozing people who disagree with her. Setting your faith boundaries and deciding what and when you'll stand up for your faith is one thing; learning how to disagree with compassion and kindness is something completely different. We need a healthy balance.

Take a moment and say a prayer to God. Thank Him for putting you in a place of influence and ask Him for wisdom to make wise choices.

"Everything in life stems from our walk with God. We need our own, everyday, walking-around friendship with God. Just Him." – Mark Hall, Casting Crowns

Lydia: Bold Steps, Brave Faith

Now let's take a trip back in time to first-century Macedonia in a city called Philippi, the ruins of which still stand in modern-day Turkey.

Philippi was a major city for trade in the ancient world, mostly because of its strategic location as a colony within the Roman Empire. But even though the city was a Roman colony, the culture within seems to have been a bit of a mixed bag. Some worshiped Caesar, as Rome declared. Others clung to the Greek heritage of many gods. Then there was a small community of God-followers, and that's where we meet a woman named Lydia. We find her story in Acts 16.

Look up Acts 16:13-15.
Where was Lydia from?

_____

What did she sell?

_____

Where did she invite the missionaries to stay?

_____

Lydia is another example. She had to find balance between her responsibilities at home, career, business, and following the mission of Christ.

What do you struggle with the most when you are striving to find balance?

_____

Describe a time in your life when you found yourself doing something you never thought you would do at a place in life where you never thought you would be?

_____

_____

Lydia is another example of humble boldness. Culturally, it wasn't okay for her to run a business, to own her home, to have employees, but she did it anyway. She didn't use her power and influence to hurt other people. She used her position to help others, no matter what the detractors in her life might have said.

God's Word can guide us on what to do to find balance and direction.

Look up the following verses and write down the promises God makes with each one:

Proverbs 1:33

_____

Isaiah 30:21

_____

Isaiah 48:17

_____

Which one of these verses is speaking to your heart and life today?

_____

When God created the world, He gave us boundaries so that we would know where we could stand and where we shouldn't. Then Jesus told us how to live, what to believe, and why.

"Don't get so busy making a living that you forget to make a life." – Dolly Parton

The world around us will change. It always has. It never believes the same thing from one moment to the next. All it takes for a massive cultural shift is a social revolution or—in today's vernacular—a Tweet that goes viral.

But God's Word never changes. He is the one constant in our lives, and if we focus on setting up and living out the boundaries He has declared are important, we'll discover a sense of balance like we've never known before. It isn't easy to set new boundaries, but the journey is well worth the distance.

Select your favorite verse from Day 3 then flip forward to Day 5 of this chapter and record it in the top box. For the rest of today spend time in prayer meditating and living out the verse you selected.

A Prayer

Heavenly Father, my life has turned upside down and inside out. I need Your help to set new boundaries and find balance. When I think about the changes I need to make, I am paralyzed with fear and overwhelmed. I'm fighting with my past failures and mess-ups. Please, God, forgive me. Erase those old, painful memories. Give me a new hope and fresh start at setting new boundaries. No matter what comes my way, I choose to believe Your promises and approach Your throne of grace with confidence. Thank You ahead of time for guiding me when I set the boundaries You have planned for me. In the name of Jesus. Amen.

Day 4: "No" Isn't a Dirty Word

When my kids were little, I wasn't just a soccer mom. I was a soccer-baseball-softball-ballet mom, and I was exhausted. We had just moved again. My children (ages 8, 11, and 13) were living in their third state, and I felt so guilty for uprooting them, I allowed them to do whatever school activities they wanted.

My two sons joined the soccer and baseball teams. My daughter chose softball and ballet, a girl after her mom's heart. But no matter how badly I wanted to accommodate them all, the schedule wasn't sustainable. But, boy, did I try.

My older son had two games and four practices every week. My middle son had two games and four practices every week. My daughter had one game, one practice, and one ballet class every week. Do that math. That's sixteen events every week. And since my husband traveled for work, the responsibility for getting them to practices, performances, and games fell solely on my shoulders. Something had to give. I needed boundaries, and God got my attention in a pretty drastic way.

I had picked up my older son from his game and was driving across town to get my daughter from her game. This was in the era before cell phones, so there was no way to communicate that Joanna had taken a softball to the face.

When I arrived to pick up my daughter, I found her with a broken nose, and someone else was taking care of her because I hadn't been there.

The guilt overwhelmed me. I gathered her up and rushed her to the hospital, feeling like the world's worst mom, like I'd failed as a parent.

Once we got to the emergency room, we encountered a boy who'd been hit in the face with a baseball. His injuries were dramatically worse than Joanna's were. Not that you ever want to take a ball to the face, but if you do, a softball will do far less damage than a baseball.

As we sat there together, I heard God whisper: "It's not that bad. Just relax. You're going to be okay."

But that was my wake-up call.

We had a family powwow that day, and after the summer, we changed things up. I restricted my kids to one sport per season. It was a difficult change to make, but I held my ground. Additionally, I chose one adult from their teams to be their "game mom" if I couldn't be there for some reason, that way I knew the person taking care of them. If I were chauffeuring kids across the city and something happened, I knew I had someone in the dugout who could hold my kid until I got there.

Now, granted, even with each kid only participating in one sport, I still had three games a week along with all the associated practices, but I had set the boundaries of what I could do. I had done what I could, and I had balanced my fears.

As a result, I experienced peace instead of anxiety.

Can you relate? Describe one of your own horror stories.

_____

_____

_____

Making the right choices

Jesus faced conflict every moment of His extraordinary life, whether it came from loved ones, antagonistic religious leaders, or the adoring crowds that never left Him alone. How did He manage?

First of all, He didn't make a habit of doing everything people told Him to do. You realize that, right? Somewhere in our genuine desire to be like Jesus, to have a servant's heart, we have developed this concept that saying no is the same as disliking someone. This idea has permeated culture to the place where self-care has become selfish.

Jesus was a servant, yes, but He still took care of Himself. When people and situations tried to draw Him into conflict, He didn't always respond, and when He did respond, He didn't do it in a way people expected.

Why do we feel obligated to say "YES" so quickly?

When did "NO" become a dirty word?

It's time to change our thinking. Our identity isn't in what we do but who we are in Christ and how we live for Him.

Four reasons how saying "NO" helps you:
1. Saying "NO" gives me room for the unexpected and/or divine opportunities from God.
2. Saying "NO" gives me room to rest and fully enjoy all my "YES" decisions.
3. Saying "NO" helps me acknowledge that I am not created to fill every need presented to me.
4. Saying "NO" makes room for someone else to say "YES."

Just Say No!
Write each of the four reasons in one of the individual boxes in the square.

Then, select one you will work on this week and circle it with your pencil.

At the end of one week, return to this page and circle the next reason you want to work on.

Return to this page when you need reminders of your reasons to say no!

Jesus had His priorities sorted out. He knew it was important to talk to people. He knew it was important to help people. That's why He was here. But He never let His mission become more important than His relationship with the One who sent Him.

Jesus knew that His power came from God, and He never compromised time with His Father.

Describe and share with your mentor what you do and when you meet with Jesus for personal quiet time?

_____

Jesus is right here with us. So how about you take a moment and tell Him what's on your heart. He wants to hear from you. Even if it's just five minutes, spend it with Him.

> Take a moment and pray. What do you need to say "No!" to this week? Use this moment to seek God's guidance and help.

The Danger Zone

If you don't set up boundaries and find balance in your life, you won't know when you're entering a danger zone. Do you know what happens next? Burn out.

You'll wear yourself out to the point where you can't function anymore. You'll lose interest in things you used to be passionate about. You'll stop caring because you've been operating beyond your limits for too long.

Everybody burns out. But nobody has to. Jesus never burned out. Do you know why?

The Bible gives us so much information about how Jesus lived that we really need to take advantage of it. We always talk about What Would Jesus Do, but how many of us actually do it?

Let's look at some examples from His life.

Read Matthew 26:36-38.
What action did He take?

_____

Who did Jesus take with Him?

_____

What did He ask them to do?

_____

Read Mark 1:35-38.
What action did He take?

_____

What is His purpose or focus?

_____

Where did Jesus go?

_____

What did He do?

_____

Read Mark 14:35-36.
What did Jesus want God to do?

_____

What did Jesus want to happen?

_____

Read Luke 6:12-16.
What action did He take?

_____

Who did He name?

_____

What is Jesus doing?

_____

Why?

_____

Read John 11:1-6.
What's wrong with Lazarus?

_____

What do Mary and Martha want Jesus to do?

_____

What does Jesus do instead?

_____

Read John 12:1-2.
What action did He take?

_____

Who is with Him?

_____

What's happening in this verse?

_____

"Down through the years, I turned to the Bible and found in it all that I needed." - Ruth Graham

Jesus made time for God in His day. He ate healthy meals. He took naps. Seriously, a lot of naps. Even when He was on a boat in the middle of a hurricane, His disciples found Him snoozing away. Jesus knew it was all right to cry and mourn. And, Jesus did a lot of walking.

Personally I'm a strong supporter of walking. Jesus did it all the time. And He was never alone either. If He weren't walking with His friends, He was walking with God.

Let's dig into Matthew 5:37. Write out what God wrote for us to set our boundaries and balance.

_____

_____

Sometimes in life, we face situations that are so difficult and exhausting that it would be impossible to attempt overcoming them alone. In these circumstances where the weight of our troubles is so excessive, the Body of Christ must come alongside and help us.

Select your favorite verse from Day 4 then flip forward to Day 5 of this chapter and record it in the top box. For the rest of today spend time in prayer meditating and living out the verse you selected.

A Prayer

Jesus, speak to me today in a mighty way. You are my Savior. I hate to admit it, but I struggle with control. I know I should give You control, but that doesn't come naturally to me. Help me seek You first and walk in Your paths. I really struggle with boundaries and balance, and I know I can't do this alone. Please, Lord, send help. Is there someone who can walk alongside me? I need a godly influence who is willing to do life together. I believe in Your Word and Your promises. I know You will supply my every need. Help me learn to say "yes" to the things You have selected for me. I'm leaning on You for strength and courage to make the right choices. Amen!

Day 5: Balance Follows Boundaries

As you complete each daily section of this study, write down a verse from each day that resonated with you.

Day 1: _____

Day 2: _____

Day 3: _____

Day 4: _____

Journal the Journey:

1. Learning to say "no" can be hard. Practice writing out what you would say to someone or something on your list as you set new boundaries.
2. Can you see how easy it can be to get caught feeling guilty about your schedule? Write out a few things you plan to change this week in your schedule in a prayer.
3. Describe your best "yes" for this week and where you can see God working in your life.

A Prayer

Dear Lord, my life is in Your hands. I have nothing left but to trust You and be restored. Today is a new day. I long to hear Your voice. I need Your direction for my schedule. Only You can deliver me and help me with my fears. Speak to my heart and change me. Teach me how to manage my time for Your glory. Turn my tears and exhaustion into laughter and joy. Don't leave my side. I need You more than ever before. I'm desperate to hear from You. Hear my cries for help, O Lord. Amen!

Mentoring Tip: The blessings come when you cross the finish line with someone by your side. Don't do life alone.

CONVERSATION 6

How Can I Hope in God
When I Feel Hopeless?

May the God of hope fill you with all joy and peace as you trust in him, so that you may overflow with hope by the power of the Holy Spirit. Romans 15:13 (NIV)

Day 1: When Your Hope Fails

Outdoor weddings seem to be the norm in my family. Many of the kids, nieces, and nephews wanted to say their vows in an outside venue, which is great and can be beautiful, but it does pose a potential problem. If the weather is bad, the wedding may end up being memorable for the wrong reasons. Ever try to run in a rain-soaked wedding dress? You won't get very far.

So for every wedding we held outside, all of us held our breath until it was over, hoping against hope that the rain would stay far away from us. Nobody wanted to go to plan B, a less-than-lovely indoor option.

We all encounter situations like this in everyday life, though. We face a major decision and make the best choice possible, and as we're going through with it, we think, "I hope this works out."

Let's face it. Sometimes it does work out, and sometimes it doesn't.

When it doesn't, and I'm facing a mess, I tell God exactly what I'm feeling: "Hey, this isn't what I hoped for. This isn't how I hoped my life would be."

Have you ever felt stuck in the middle of a life you hadn't hoped for?

_____

For me, one of my greatest hopes was for my parents to get to meet and love on all my grandchildren. To have four generations of my family in one room at a time would have been the greatest blessing I could have imagined. I had hoped to see my mother as a great-grandma, pouring into all of my grandchildren. She was full of life and fun and brought joy into every room she entered. But that wasn't what God had in mind.

Can we be honest? Was there ever a time in your life you cried out to God with a loud "Why, Lord?" How did you face those feelings and emotions?

_____

Why do you think God didn't give you what you hoped for?

_____

Maybe you didn't get the job you wanted. Maybe the house you wanted to buy got sold to someone else. Maybe your family refused to gather for a holiday. And maybe it didn't make sense to you at the moment, but God has a way of redeeming those lost hopes.

Do you believe in Romans 8:28? "For all things work together for good to those who love the Lord." Let's reflect back on the things that you hoped for but didn't receive. List the top three difficult situations and what you learned about God and yourself through that situation.

Difficult Situation	Romans 8:28 Lesson Learned
1.	1.
2.	2.
3.	3.

As you read Romans 8:28, what confidence can you have as a follower of Christ about the situations that occur in your life?

_____

Today, how have you seen the Lord bring good out of a bad situation?

When we follow Jesus, we can experience true hope. True hope is **expecting with confidence that God will fulfill His promises to us**.

That doesn't mean we ask God to turn the sky green and the grass purple and expect Him to do it. We don't ask Him to fulfill promises He never made. But it does mean we should know what He's promised.

People who belong to the world won't understand this kind of hope. To someone who has never met Jesus, it won't make any logical sense to them. But for us who know Jesus personally, hope is our bread and butter.

> It is my deepest desire that every person reading this book will have a fresh encounter with the promises of God and grow to know Him more as their God of hope.

> Psalm 146:5 tells us, "Happy are those who are helped by the God of Jacob. Their hope is in the LORD their God. He made heaven and earth, the sea and everything in it. He remains loyal forever."

Remind yourself today of who God is. Say this out loud:

"God is my hope. He always keeps His promises."

Days will come where you feel like God has left you alone. He hasn't. Hold on to hope in Him.

The Promises of God

There are more than 4,000 promises of God in the Bible for those who follow Christ. Here is a short list of 66 of them, one from each book of the Bible. As you read each one of these promises, highlight the ones that are important to you today.

OLD TESTAMENT

- GENESIS 18:14 – Nothing is too hard for the Lord.
- EXODUS 33:14 – My presence will go with you.
- LEVITICUS 26:11 – I will live among you and be your God.
- NUMBERS 14:18 – The Lord is slow to anger, abounding in love and forgiving sin.
- DEUTERONOMY 3:22 – The Lord your God Himself will fight for you.
- JOSHUA 23:14 – Every promise has been fulfilled; not one has failed.
- JUDGES 6:12 – The Lord is with you; mighty warrior.
- RUTH 4:14 – Praise be to the Lord, who this day has not left you without a kinsman-redeemer.
- 1 SAMUEL 2:30 – Those who honor me I will honor.
- 2 SAMUEL 22:31 – As for God, his way is perfect; the word of the Lord is flawless.
- 1 KINGS 8:23 – O Lord, God of Israel, there is no God like you in heaven above or earth below
- 2 KINGS 5:15 – There is no God in all the world except in Israel.
- 1 CHRONICLES 16:34 – Give thanks to the Lord, for he is good; his love endures forever.
- 2 CHRONICLES 16:9 – The eyes of the Lord range throughout the earth to strengthen those whose hearts are fully committed to him.
- EZRA 8:22 – The gracious hand of our God is on everyone who looks to him.
- NEHEMIAH 8:10 – The joy of the Lord is your strength.
- ESTHER 4:14 – If you remain silent at this time, relief and delivery will arise from another place.
- JOB 19:25 – I know that my Redeemer lives.
- PSALM 55:22 – Cast your cares on the Lord and he will sustain you.
- PROVERBS 16:3 – Commit to the Lord whatever you do and He will establish your plans.
- ECCLESIASTES 3:11 – He has made everything beautiful in its time.

- SONG OF SONGS 2:4 – He has taken me to the banquet hall, and his banner over me is love.
- ISAIAH 26:3 – You will keep in perfect peace those whose minds are steadfast, because they trust in you.
- JEREMIAH 1:5 – Before I formed you in the womb I knew you, before you were born I set you apart.
- LAMENTATIONS 3:32 – Though he brings grief, he will show compassion.
- EZEKIEL 36:26 – I will give you a new heart and put a new spirit in you.
- DANIEL 9:4 – The Lord, the great and awesome God, who keeps his covenant of love with those who love him and keep his commandments.
- HOSEA 6:6 – I desire mercy, not sacrifice.
- JOEL 2:25 – I will repay you for the years the locusts have eaten.
- AMOS 3:7 – Surely the Sovereign Lord does nothing without revealing his plan to his servant.
- OBADIAH 1:15 – The day of the Lord is near for all nations.
- JONAH 2:2 – In my distress I called to the Lord, and He answered me.
- MICAH 6:8 – What does the Lord require of you, "To act justly and to love mercy and to walk humbly with your Lord."
- NAHUM 1:7 – The Lord is good, a refuge in times of trouble. He cares for those who trust in him.
- HABAKKUK 1:13 – Your eyes are too pure to look on evil; You cannot tolerate wrong.
- ZEPHANIAH 3:17 – He will rejoice over you with singing.
- HAGGAI 2:6 – This is what the Lord Almighty says: "In a little while once more shake the heavens and the earth, the sea and the day land. I will shake all nations, and the desired of all nations will come and I will fill this house with glory."
- ZECHARIAH 2:8 – Whoever touches you touches the apple of his eye.
- MALACHI 3:6-7 – I the Lord do not change…Return to me, and I will return to you.

NEW TESTAMENT

- MATTHEW 11:28 – Come to me, all you who are weary and heavy laden and I will give you rest.
- MARK 2:1-12 – Jesus offers the glorious gift of the forgiveness of sins.
- LUKE 18:1-8 – When we persevere in prayer, God will answer our petitions.
- JOHN 1:12 – Yet to all who did receive him, to those who believed in his name, he gave the right to become children of God.
- ACTS 17:27-28 – God is not far from each one of us, for in him we live and move and have our being.
- ROMANS 12:2 – God's will is—his good, pleasing and perfect will.
- 1 CORINTHIANS 1:2 – He made you holy by means of Christ Jesus, just as he did for all people everywhere.
- 2 CORINTHIANS 5:17 – If anyone is in Christ, he is a new creation.
- GALATIANS 1:3-4 – Christ Jesus gave himself for our sins to rescue us from the present evil age.
- EPHESIANS 3:20 – God is able to do immeasurably more than all we ask or imagine, according to the power that is at work within us.
- PHILIPPIANS 1:6 – He who began a good work in us will carry it on to completion until the day of Christ Jesus.
- COLOSSIANS 1:27 – The riches of God's mystery are Christ in us, the hope of glory
- 1 THESSALONIANS 4:16 – The Lord himself will come down from heaven.
- 2 THESSALONIANS 1:5-10 – God will ultimately reward all believers who suffer for the sake of the gospel.
- 1 TIMOTHY 1:15 – Christ Jesus came into the world to save sinners.
- 2 TIMOTHY 1:7 – God did not give us a spirit of timidity, but a spirit of power, of love and a sound mind.
- TITUS 2:14 – We wait for the blessed hope.

- PHILEMON 25 – The grace of the Lord Jesus Christ is with our spirits.
- HEBREWS 4:12 – the word of God is living and active.
- JAMES 1:17 – Every good and perfect gift is from above.
- 1 PETER 5:7 – Cast all your anxiety on him because he cares for you.
- 2 PETER 1:4 – He has given us great and precious promises.
- 1 JOHN 1:2 – God is light; in him there is no darkness at all.
- 2 JOHN 1:2 – The truth of the gospel of Jesus Christ "lives in us and will be with us forever."
- 3 JOHN 1:11 – Anyone who does what is good is from God.
- JUDE 1:24 – To him who is able to keep you from stumbling and to present you before his glorious presence without fault and with great joy.
- REVELATION 1:3 – God will bless everyone who reads this prophecy to others, and he will bless everyone who hears and obeys it because the time is almost near.

Lessons from Paul

Look up 2 Corinthians 11:24-27 using the English Standard Version (ESV) and write Paul's many trials in the blanks below:

_____ times the Jewish leaders gave him _____ lashes.

_____ times he was beaten with _____.

_____ he was stoned.

_____ times he was shipwrecked.

_____ he spent _____ adrift at sea.

Faced dangers from _____ and _____.

Faced dangers from his people, both _____ and _____.

Face dangers in _____, _____, and _____.

Has been _____ many nights.

Has been _____ and _____.

Has been _____ without clothing.

Have you ever known one person to have endured so much trauma and pain and horror? Paul did.

As the first missionary, Paul traveled all around Europe and Asia in the first century. Some scholars believe that he made it all the way to first-century Great Britain—from Israel. And it wasn't exactly like he could board an airplane and arrive in a few hours. Paul had to travel by boat, horse, donkey, wagon, and foot. Quite an extraordinary story for someone who began his life exterminating Christians, right?

Now look back at that same passage and read 2 Corinthians 11:30. Fill in the blanks.

If I must boast, I would rather boast about _____.

Does that make any sense at all? How could Paul be so happy to rejoice in the most damaging and difficult parts of his life?

Why is Paul so happy and upbeat even though his circumstances and experiences were so horrific and difficult? You and I will never experience the difficulties Paul experienced and yet, he is still able to maintain his joyful hope. How is that possible?

How could Paul be joyful in hope in spite of being in hopeless situations?

Paul placed his hope in God and not in a person or thing on this earth. Paul based his joy and hope on his faith in God's promises. When we are facing difficult situations we can only find hope when we know the God of hope.

Paul had true hope. He knew God never disappoints the one who hopes in Him. He knew he could trust in the God who created everything. And so can we.

Be joyful in hope. Romans 12:12

Read the following verses and write the Scripture references (ESV) along side of the triangle that belong together.

Colossians 1:23	Psalm 25:21	Titus 1:2
1 Thessalonians 1:3	Psalm 31:24	Job 13:15
1 Thessalonians 5:8	Jeremiah 14:22	Lamentations 3:25

Claim your Hope triangle to start living with a joyful hope in God.

"Outside of the cross of Jesus Christ, there is no hope in this world. That cross and resurrection at the core of the Gospel is the only hope for humanity." - Ravi Zacharias

Select your favorite verse from Day 1 then flip forward to Day 5 of this chapter and record it in the top box. For the rest of today spend time in prayer meditating and living out the verse you selected.

A Prayer

Oh, God, I know you are a good God. The Scripture tells me that is true. But, just being honest right now, this doesn't feel good. Why is this happening? I've been broken for so long and just really need relief. I confess I feel forgotten. It seems like I'm alone and forever waiting on You to move in my life. I know You are with me, but I'm tired of drifting and want to be anchored in Your hope. Please, God, help me have a stronger hope in You. I need You more than ever, and I'm placing all my hope in You and crying out to You. You are the God of my hope. Amen!

Day 2: Impossible Hope, Impossible God
Lisa Beamer: A Heart Prepared for Hope

When Lisa Beamer was 15 years old, her father died of an aneurysm. Her family had no warning, no indication that he was even ill. That's often how aneurysms work. Lisa, already a committed Christ-follower in her teenage years, faced the rest of her life without her dad.

"When my father died, faith wasn't so easy anymore. . . . I spent five years asking why, expressing my anger saying it's not fair, before God helped me realize that He is who He is all the time – in good circumstances and bad. He is all-powerful and all-loving, but that doesn't mean that as a citizen of this fallen world he protects us from every 'bad' event."[17]

In the emotional turmoil following her father's death, Lisa found comfort and hope in a passage of Scripture, but it might not be the one you're expecting.

Look up Romans 11:33-36 and read it to yourself. Then, summarize this passage in the space below:

_____

_____

_____

Oh, the depth of the riches of the wisdom and knowledge of God!

It's not a passage about comfort or hope. The point of it isn't to remind people where their loved ones have gone after death. It's a brief statement on who God is and why we can trust Him.

Isn't that what we need to know if we're going to discover hope? Lisa Beamer thought so.

This passage gave her comfort and helped her through the loss and grief of her father's untimely death, but at the time, she couldn't have imagined (not even in her worst nightmares) how this passage would reappear in her life when she needed it again.

Seventeen years later, Lisa Beamer was 32 with two sons and a third child on the way, and she became a widow when her husband Todd became the hero of United Flight 93, which crashed in Pennsylvania on 9/11.

If you've heard the phrase, "Let's roll" in association with September 11, you've heard Todd's last recorded words, uttered as he led the attack on the terrorists who had hijacked their flight.

Before the horror of that day, Lisa had been studying for a class she was to teach on Esther, and the Lord led her back to Romans 11:33-36. This beautiful passage on God's sovereignty seemed to mesh well with what Lisa planned to present to the class, but she didn't understand how she would need the promise of this passage only a few days later.

Shortly after the crash of United Flight 93, the FBI released Todd's vehicle from where it had been impounded in a search for evidence. In Todd's belongings removed from the vehicle, Lisa found something that took her breath away—Scripture memory cards Todd used during his drive time. And the top card, the one he would have been memorizing on September 11, was Romans 11:33-36.[18]

Oh, the depth of the riches of the wisdom and knowledge of God!

The same passage that brought her comfort in her father's death, the same passage the Lord gave her to teach a few days earlier, was the same passage God had given her husband only hours before he left this earth.

When we suffer, when our hearts are broken in two, when the worst has happened and we feel lost, we cannot understand what God is doing. Not then. We aren't big enough to see all the pieces of His plan or how they can possibly fit together to make something good.

But God can. And in His view, in His kindness, in His power, one difficult situation may be preparing you for another.

"Slowly I began to understand that the plans God has for us don't just include 'good' things ... I remember my mom saying that many people look for miracles — things that in their human minds 'fix' a difficult situation. Many miracles, however, are not a change to the normal course of human events; they're found in God's ability and desire to sustain and nurture people through even the worst situations. Somewhere along the way, I stopped demanding that God fix the problems in my life and started to be thankful for his presence as I endured them." —Lisa Beamer, Let's Roll![19]

The truth is, God takes care of us now. He's here in our present suffering and trials, not just later in life. Whatever you're enduring today, He cares, He knows, He sees.

Like Lisa Beamer, it's time to see the struggles in your life today for what they really are — evidence that God's not through with you yet, that God hasn't given up on you. So don't give up on Him.

Learning to trust the God of Hope is a process. Like any other relationship, it takes time, communication, and proof before you can honestly, genuinely trust God's direction in your life, so don't think it can happen overnight.

On a scale of 1 to 10, how much do you think you trust God today? Be honest.

What would you need to trust God more?

_____

Have you asked God to provide that need?

_____

 Take a moment and talk to Jesus about the need you wrote down. Whatever it is, whatever stands between you and God, ask Jesus to help you.

Jonathan: The Power of Hope

Ever met a crown prince? If you have, I hope you got a photograph. Most of us commoners will never have an opportunity to meet royalty, not in this life at least. But if there were one prince I wanted to meet, it would have been Jonathan.

His dad, not so much.

Jonathan was the son of King Saul, the first king of Israel. Saul, I'm sure, had great plans for Jonathan, had likely envisioned the family line extending for generation after generation. But God had something better in mind.

We're going to talk about an epic action scene in Scripture, so go read 1 Samuel 14:1-15. Be ready to talk about this, because it's wild.

> Jonathan wasn't out causing trouble. The Philistines and the people of Israel were at war, and God had commanded that Israel chase the Philistines out of the land. They weren't supposed to be there, and Jonathan took it on himself to lead the battle.

"Let's go across to the outpost of those pagans," **Jonathan said to his armor bearer. "Perhaps the LORD** **will help us, for nothing can hinder the LORD. He can** **win a battle whether he has many warriors or only a** **few!" 1 Samuel 14:5-6 (NLT)**

What does this passage tell you about Jonathan's trust in God?

_____

Look at 1 Samuel 14:4 and write the names of the cliffs in the spaces provided: _____ & _____

Bozez means *Slippery.*
Seneh means *Thorny.*
Would you like to climb a cliff with either of those names?
I wouldn't. That just sounds painful.

The cliffs that Jonathan had to climb weren't little hills. They were rocky, treacherous, dangerous piles of boulders and thorns. Climbing up them to fight a superior force at the top is a crazy idea. But Jonathan clearly understood what God wanted him to do—something impossible.

Nothing slowed Jonathan down. Nothing stopped him from what he knew God had asked of him. Jonathan believed with every fiber of his soul that God would keep His promises.

Take a closer look at 1 Samuel 14:12-13.

Who accompanied Jonathan on this mission? _____

What did they use to climb the cliff? _____ and _____

Jonathan had a friend along for the ride, someone who had vowed to stand beside him through thick and thin. No matter what Jonathan did or where he went, his friend would go with him. We all need someone like that in our lives.

After climbing "Slippery" and "Thorny," Jonathan and his armor bearer were probably exhausted. They likely had scrapes on their knees and elbows, maybe even thorns in their skin, but they couldn't relax at the top. They had to go into battle. And, boy, did they go into battle.

Read verse 14 and write down how many enemy soldiers Jonathan and his armor-bearer killed: _____

That's valor worthy of a superhero, don't you think? For two men to do that kind of damage to an army of men? It would have been impossible if God hadn't been with them, if Jonathan hadn't believed without question.

Then what happened? Did these two heroes have to fight the entire army all by themselves? Write what happened in your own words in the space provided:

_____

_____

For a second, put yourself in the shoes of these enemy soldiers. Philistines were scary people. They lived for battles and conquest and bloody victories. They were known across the Middle East for their cruelty and their might in battle.

So what would they have thought when two puny little Israelite soldiers scrambled up a steep, dangerous cliff to challenge them in battle? Well, we know what they said. Check out verse 12 and fill in the blank:

1 Samuel 14:12 _____

Ha-ha. Yes. Funny. Until the fighting started. And those two puny

Hebrews slaughtered twenty of their men, and it didn't stop there. Because the ground started shaking. Panic tore through their lines, and even the bravest, most valiant Philistine warrior ended up trembling in terror, not only in the camp where Jonathan and his armor-bearer were fighting, but also out in the fields, the outposts, and the raiding parties.

They were so terrified, they started fighting each other.

Impossible, right?

That's kind of the point.

Jonathan didn't rely on his royal status for success and victory. He didn't trust in the name of his father, the King of Israel. He didn't even lean on his own prowess in combat, which was significant. No, Jonathan had little faith in himself, but he had great, unshakable faith in God. Jonathan never encountered a hopeless situation, because he truly believed God could do anything.

In comparison to Jonathan's response to obstacles, how do you respond to the challenges you face in your life?

_____

What cliffs do you think God is calling you to climb?

_____

Being gut-honest, what would it take for your walk with God to be called trusting and confident?

_____

The cliffs that Jonathan and his armor-bearer climbed were called "Slippery" and "Thorny." What are the cliffs in your path called? Write their names on the mountain image below.

Why did you name your mountain cliffs the way you did?

_____

_____

_____

You will never find hope by accident. If you want to find hope, you have to search for it. You have to be intentional about who you trust, who you listen to, and who you follow. It's a process, and it's not only your life on the line.

When you learn how to hope, you have an effect on the people around you.

Jonathan was farther down the road in his hope and faith. Did you notice this in the story we just read? He'd walked a little farther in his faith journey than his friend, so he took the time and the opportunity to share his experience and mentor his friend about trusting in the God of hope.

Is there someone in your life who needs hope? Has God put a younger friend in your path who you could experience the power of God's hope with? It doesn't take much to walk alongside someone else, especially if you're on the same journey. Share your struggles. Share your fears. Climb those cliffs together, and together you can see for yourself that God is faithful, and He always keeps His promises.

Select your favorite verse from Day 2 then flip forward to Day 5 of this chapter and record it in the top box. For the rest of today spend time in prayer meditating and living out the verse you selected.

A Prayer

Heavenly Father, I'm at a total loss for words. Sometimes I feel like I'm drowning in sadness and confusion. My head says one thing, and my heart tells me another. I want to live with hope in You like Lisa and so many others have, but I can't do it alone. I need Your help. I desperately want to trust You with my hurts and pain, so I can finally turn around and give help to another person. Do whatever it takes to change my life and stretch me into a stronger believer full of hope in You, so I can share my story with others. Amen!

Day 3: Beyond Our Understanding

Do you need to understand something before you trust it?

Ideally, yes. It's difficult to trust a person or a process if you don't understand it, but in some cases (more than we'd like to admit, likely) we don't have a choice.

Our beautiful blue planet spins at a ridiculous rate of about 1,000 miles an hour. We can't feel it, though, because we are traveling through space at the same rate, glued on to Earth's muddy surface by an unseen, invisible force called Gravity.

If you believe the stories, Sir Isaac Newton realized gravity was a thing when he saw an apple fall from a tree. He started asking questions, and many of his questions have yet to be answered. Because, believe it or not, science still can't actually explain what gravity is or where it comes from or why some planets have it and others don't.

But we know it's there. We see evidence of it every day. We experience its effects every day. And we can trust that if we lose our grip on a cup of coffee, gravity will cause it to fall to the floor and splatter everywhere.

No, we're not going to have a lesson in physics and quantum mechanics, but what we need to realize is how frequently we all trust in something we don't understand.

You do it. I do it. Everyone firmly believes in gravity, yet none of us can explain it.

Keyword Study & Simple Steps
Romans 11:33-36

Part 1: "How impossible it is for us to understand his decisions and his ways!" (v. 33b)
#1: Impossible
1. Write Webster's definition for the word *impossible*:

_____

2. The Bible overflows with stories of how God has accomplished impossible things for His people, both in the Old Testament and the New Testament. God constantly reminds us that what is impossible for Man is possible with God.

Is God stretching you right now? What impossible thoughts were you entertaining before you started Conversation 6? Are you willing to move from impossible to possible-with-God right now?

#2: Understand

1. When you need to understand a subject or a topic of discussion, what do you do?

_____

_____

2. Sometimes studying isn't enough to understand. Sometimes you must ask an expert or a mentor before you can truly grasp its meaning.

3. Some aspects of God, we will never understand, because God's ways are not our ways and God's thoughts are not our thoughts.

How did Paul describe the mind of God in this verse? Do you have a tough decision to make? What hope statements or Scriptures have you learned this week to help you make a wise choice?

_____

#3: Decisions and Ways

1. Using a dictionary, define the difference between the words *decisions* and *ways*:

_____

_____

2. In the original Greek language, the word for *decisions* is translated *judgments*. The text indicates that God's judgments are unsearchable (or "cannot be searched into"). Using the logic and reason that Mankind has available to understand why God does what He does will end in failure and frustration. The only tool we have that can reveal God's thoughts is Scripture itself.

3. In the original Greek language, the text says that God's ways are untraceable (or "cannot be traced out"). This is a similar statement. No matter how well we may be able to navigate the storms of our lives, we cannot predict what God will do next, but thanks to Scripture, we know that whatever God chooses to do will be good.

Take a moment and thank Jesus for what He's done in your life. You may not be able to understand it all yet, but because you can trust Him, you can know that He's working everything out for your good and His glory.

Part 2: "For everything comes from him and exists by his power and is intended for his glory." (v. 36a)

#4: Exists

1. What is God's place in the universe? _____

2. Another translation of verse 36 reads as follows:

> "For **from Him** and **through Him** and **to Him** are all things. To Him be the glory forever. Amen."

Describe what is from God, through God, and to God:

_____

3. What is the difference between the way God exists and the way humans exist?

_____

#5: Intended

1. The word *intended* sometimes requires context to understand its meaning. In the English language, *intended* can mean anything from a person you're supposed to marry to a direction for the mind. In this context, "intended for glory" means that all creation was designed for the specific purpose of bringing glory to God.

2. In the original Greek, verse 36 tells us that all things are From, Through, and Unto (or For) God.

3. If you believed your past, your whole existence, your entire purpose in life was to bring glory to God, how differently would you live?

_____

We can't always understand, but we can still trust.

How is that possible? It's easy, if it's someone you know.

Men and women don't always understand each other. Siblings don't always understand each other. Friends don't always understand each other. None of us are mind-readers, and we certainly aren't soul-readers. So in those instances where we don't understand, we have to trust what we know for sure. The same is true in our relationship with God.

How do we know who God is?

Look up the verses and write down what each verse tells us about God.

Exodus 34:6

_____

Numbers 23:19

_____

Deuteronomy 4:31

_____

Psalm 94:22

_____

Matthew 22:32

_____

John 4:24

_____

Acts 10:34

_____

Romans 5:5

_____

1 Corinthians 1:9

_____

1 John 1:5

_____

1 John 4:16

_____

Read Psalm 3:2-6 (NLT) and fill in the blanks:

_____

So many are saying, "God will _____ him! But you, O Lord, are a _____ around me; you are _____ _____, the one who _____ _____ _____ high. I cried out to the Lord, and _____ me from his holy mountain. I _____ _____ and _____, for the Lord was _____ _____ _____. I am not _____ of ten thousand enemies who _____ me on every side."

(NLT)

Because we know who God is and what He's promised, we can trust Him. And if we can trust Him, we have every reason to hope.

As long as the sun comes up in the morning, there is still hope. God is our hope.

What will you trust God with today?

"Hope sees the invisible, feels the intangible and achieves the impossible. Optimism is the faith that leads to achievement. Nothing can be done without hope and confidence." - Helen Keller

Select your favorite verse from Day 3 then flip forward to Day 5 of this chapter and record it in the top box. For the rest of today spend time in prayer meditating and living out the verse you selected.

A Prayer

Lord Jesus, I don't understand what You are doing, but I'm learning to trust You in it anyway. Sometimes all I have is just a little faith, but I'm learning that's all I need. I'm going to trust You with everything I've got because You are able to rescue me. And even if You don't, I'm still placing my hope in You. Thank You, Jesus, for coming to this Earth to save sinners like me. I've been rescued from the pit. On my own, my life would be a disaster, but praise the Lord I am no longer alone. I have You, my Savior and Redeemer. I believe, all things work together for good for those who love the Lord, and I love You, Lord. Amen!

Day 4: Your Faith in Future Tense

I have a friend who is turning 40 next year, but instead of winding down or relaxing as she nears this milestone of a birthday, she's stepping up. She set a goal to run in the Music City Marathon.

Marathon running isn't like regular running. When you think of running in a race, you think of quick sprints. One-minute miles. Usain Bolt or Jackie Joyner Kersey.

Marathons don't work that way. In case you don't know, if you're running a marathon, you're running 26.2 miles. Miles. Most people can't decide to run a marathon overnight and pull it off the next morning.

You have to train.

Experts recommend that you are already running 20-to-30 miles a week on a regular basis before you even attempt to run a marathon. Even better, they say, is to build up a weekly mileage total of 50 miles over the four months of training you need.

Beyond that, even if you were physically able to run 26.2 miles without training, you'd still likely fail because your body won't be prepared for the strain of burning so much energy so quickly. Coaches and trainers warn marathon runners that around mile markers 18 or maybe 20, they'll likely reach a place where they want to give up. This is called *hitting the wall*. The human body is only able to store so much energy before it gives out, but proper training helps the body learn how to adjust and overcome.

Do you see why this might be a big deal for my friend? It's a lot of work. It's a huge challenge, and it's not just about the physical capability. It's also emotional and mental.

She had to run every week. She had to work toward building up her stamina, adding miles every week, going further, going faster, going harder.

And she did.

Then, the unimaginable happened.

During her weekly training run, her foot started hurting. She pushed through it. It spread to her heel, specifically, and it flared up like hot spikes stabbing her every morning.

Her chiropractor informed her that she had plantar fasciitis.

If you've never experienced this excruciating level of pain, count yourself blessed. It's a condition that plagues runners, especially those who start running or walking after a period of non-activity. And there's not much you can do about it—except to stop running.

All the training, all the sacrifice, all the intense hard work she had done over a year to get her body in peak physical condition for the marathon rested on how much pain she could endure.

So my friend faced a terrible choice. She could stop, give up, turn away from all her investments in training for the marathon, or she could run anyway and hope for the best.

What would you choose?

What do you think she chose?

I want to stop here and ask a real, honest, personal question:

Have you hit a wall in your faith?

Don't feel singled out if you have. Everyone does.

But there's a deeper question beyond this one.

Have you ever wondered if you really are a Christ-follower? Do you know for sure that your name is written in the Lamb's Book of Life?

You can know for sure. You don't have to wonder any longer. Becoming a for-real Christ-follower is so simple. Asking God to be your Savior isn't complicated.

1. Tell Jesus you're broken and you need Him.

- Only His death on the cross and His resurrection can pay the price for your eternal life with Him.

The Lamb's Book of Life?

The Bible often mentions a special book kept in heaven, which records the names of every single human being who made the choice to follow Jesus.

The Bible tells us that our names are registered in heaven (Luke 10:20) and whoever's name is written in the book will be rescued (Daniel 12:1). Paul and John tell us that the book is called the Book of Life or the Lamb's Book of Life (Philippians 4:3, Revelation 21:27).

The only way to have your name written in the Lamb's Book of Life is to turn your own life over to Jesus and accept Him as your Savior, your one and only path to salvation.

- Don't be afraid. He already knows.
- But He needs to hear it from you.

2. Ask Jesus to be your Lord and Savior.

- That's all there is to it. No ritual. No magic words. Nothing you need to give or do or be. Jesus did all that for you.
- Because you can trust who He is, you can have confidence that He'll keep His promises.

Next?

Write down today's date down and place a stake in the ground. Build a memorial so you can remember the choice you made.

Then, you can walk in confidence, knowing you will never be alone again and that you'll spend eternity with Christ Himself in Heaven.

You've started off on a marvelous journey to become more like Jesus, to know God better, and to understand the incredible purpose He has for your life. The only way to learn more about God's character is to study God's Word, the Bible. So complete this study and move on to the next one. Ask another believer to walk with you, to learn with you, to share your experiences along the road.

And always talk to God. Have real, personal conversations with Him through prayer. Remember, He is your 24/7/365 best friend, and He'll never leave your side.

You can't have hope without faith. It doesn't work. But if you think about it, hope is really only your faith in future tense.

> **If we already have something, we don't need to hope for it. Romans 8:24b (NLT)**

So where does this find you today? Maybe you're struggling to see a financial dream come true. Maybe you're reeling from a surprise relocation. Maybe you feel like everything in life has just turned upside down, and you don't know where to turn.

You're not alone.

Our entire culture is drowning in a hopeless search for something solid to hold on to, and the longer we search, the more exhausted we get.

Are you weary? Are you tired of fighting those overwhelming tidal waves of hopelessness?

What do you do when you feel hopeless?

Throughout this conversation, especially back in Day 1, we talked about how Jesus is in our anchor, and He is. He keeps us stable when the currents and the waves try to carry us away. But hopelessness can be an anchor too. Feeling hopeless can keep you mired in the muck and seaweed in the shallows when you need to get somewhere.

The more hopeless you feel, the less you'll try to break free.

My friends, God made you free. So don't succumb to the power of hopelessness, not when Jesus is reaching out His mighty hand to you. All you need to do is take it. And I have three steps for you to take that will help you break loose from your hopelessness and cling to the Hope of Glory.

The Three B-Attitudes to Move from Hopeless to Hopeful

1. Begin Steady.

Begin each day on your knees and talk to God. Tell Him what you adore and appreciate about Him. Then, tell Him where you fall short and where you need Him to show up. Talk in a personal conversation with the God of the universe. He wants to have an intimate daily relationship with you. (Make sure you read the prayer at the end of this day as I demonstrate my own morning time with God to help you get started.)

Then, thank Him for what you're experiencing. Good or bad, fun or horrifying, exhilarating or exhausting—thank God in every circumstance. Thank God for the people in your life, the ones you love and the ones you don't even like.

Read 1 Thessalonians 5:18.

"Give thanks in all circumstances for this is God's will for you in Christ Jesus."

Which circumstances are you supposed to give thanks for? Only the ones that are comfortable? Only the ones that benefit you?

No. That word is ALL.

Tell God out loud that you are thankful for what's happening in your life, whether you understand it or not, because regardless if it's good or bad, God is big enough to use it. And if that's not good enough reason to be thankful, I don't know what is.

What can you thank God for right now?

---

2. Build Up.

Talk to yourself. I'm serious. Maybe not out loud, if that makes you uncomfortable, but talk to yourself about how you will trust God today. Build yourself up. Tell yourself the truth of God. Speak and think good thoughts toward yourself.

Even if you have to say to yourself, "I don't understand what's happening right now, but I trust God anyway," do it

This isn't denial. Living in denial is ignoring your problems or your circumstances, refusing to recognize that any of it exists. That's not what this is.

Building yourself up is the conscious decision to trust God in spite of your circumstances. You acknowledge the problems you're facing are too big for you to handle, but because God is God, He will work it out. You're not running away from your problems; you're turning them over to God.

> **And David was greatly distressed; for the people spake of stoning him, because the soul of all the people was grieved, every man for his sons and for his daughters: but David encouraged himself in the Lord his God.**
> **1 Samuel 30:6**

Read the full chapter of 1 Samuel 30 to understand what was happening in this verse. It's important to note that at this moment in David's life, he had no one to encourage him, so David encouraged himself in the Lord his God.

Read Proverbs 3:5-6.

"Trust in the LORD with all your heart; do not depend on your own understanding. Seek his will in all you do, and he will show you which path to take."

You won't always understand what God is doing, but you can always know that He is good. So you can trust Him.

Repeat it to yourself every day. Repeat it in your heart every moment. Use this truth to build up your hope, your dreams, and your image of yourself.

Write a personal statement to repeat to yourself the next time you start feeling hopeless:

_____

_____

_____

3. Bless Others.

Whenever I am down or feeling extremely sad, I immediately begin looking for someone else to bless. Who can I pour into? Who can help today? Who can I be a blessing to?

Approaching life with this perspective will return a blessing to you greater than one you've given to someone else.

Be active. Be mobile. Get involved in your church. Volunteer in your community. Help your neighbor mow their yard. Just do something.

Too many times, Christ-followers sit back and wait for God's will to be apparent in their lives, when all along He's waving madly at the opportunities all around us. We need to open our eyes to the needs of people in our lives.

You don't have to know everything. You don't need all the answers. You don't have to have your life all together. All you need is a willing heart.

Don't sit. Get busy. The more you invest in other people, the more you'll get to see how God is alive and active and working in peoples' hearts. And believe it or not, you'll get more hope and encouragement from the people you serve than almost anything else.

Write three names of people in your life who you can serve this week:

1. _____

2. _____

3. _____

> Stop and ask Jesus to help you as you learn to Begin Steady, Build Up, and Bless Others in your life of following Him.

What if I don't have faith?

"Hope is not a wish or a sprinkle of magical fairy dust. Hope is a person." Sarah Thacker

Read 1 Timothy 1:1 (NASB) as it's written for you below:

Paul, an apostle of Jesus Christ by the commandment of God our Savior, and of Christ Jesus, who is our hope"

Faith is hard. If you need demonstrations or physical evidence that you can touch or see, faith is going to be a difficult concept for you to grasp. But the truth is, faith is essential to hope. And you can only find hope and hold on to it by reading God's Word.

Even then, you may struggle. And that's okay. Everyone does. It's part of being human, and for many people, faith doesn't come easily. But that's because we don't really understand what faith is.

Faith isn't a warm, fuzzy feeling you experience when life is good. It isn't an emotion that tingles in your soul and leads you to lift your hands in worship. It isn't an abstract concept you can only experience when the planets align.

Faith is a choice. It's something you choose to do every morning when you wake up, rain or shine.

So if you don't have faith, act like you do.

That, in essence, is faith. It's the conscious choice to press forward with what God says is right when you don't understand, when you can't find the answers, when everything is on the line.

Once you have faith, even if you're only acting like you do, hope won't be far behind.

"God when you choose to leave mountains unmovable, give me the strength to be able to sing it is well with my soul." "Even If" MercyMe

Select your favorite verse from Day 4 then flip forward to Day 5 of this chapter and record it in the top box. For the rest of today spend time in prayer meditating and living out the verse you selected.

A Prayer

Good morning, Lord. I confess I am broken and need a Savior. I have made so many mistakes. I've heard other people talk about You in an intimate way and couldn't ever relate to their words, but today I get it. I need You. Will You come into my heart and soul and be my very best friend and Savior for every minute of every day for the rest of my life? When I take control of my life, I mess things up. Right now, I hand You my life and give You complete control today. I claim today for You and acknowledge my new personal relationship with You as my Lord and Savior. I know this long journey won't be easy, but I'm holding on to Your promise that You will never leave me or forsake me on the journey.
My heart rejoices in You. Amen!

Day 5: Living an Unshakable Life

As you complete each daily section of this study, write down your favorite verse from each day.

Day 1: _____

Day 2: _____

Day 3: _____

Day 4: _____

Journal the Journey:

1. How has your hope in Jesus Christ helped you through this week?

2. Write about a time when God showed up and did something amazing when a situation seemed hopeless.
3. Write your prayer of thanksgiving to the Lord for the new HOPE you have in Him.

A Prayer

Mighty Savior, my hope is in You and You alone. I have good intentions but not a good track record. Help me, Lord, to be consistent in meeting with You each day and getting on my knees to pray. Our prayer time together is my favorite time. I feel Your strong presence when I pray. During the moments when I struggle with trust, You help me to choose faith and hope over my doubt. Even during the dark times Your word will help me choose You over everything else. I praise You for your goodness and mercy. Amen!

Mentoring Tip: Just a few encouraging words can plant a seed of hope.

CONVERSATION 7

Where Is God When Bad Things Happen To Me?

O Lord, you have searched me and known me! You know when I sit down and when I rise up; you discern my thoughts from afar. You search out my path and my lying down and are acquainted with all my ways. Even before a word is on my tongue, behold, O Lord, you know it altogether. You hem me in, behind and before, and lay your hand upon me. Such knowledge is too wonderful for me; it is high; I cannot attain it. Psalm 139:1-6 (ESV)

Day 1: Handling Your Hurt

Adulting is so much harder than I thought it would be.

Ever thought that to yourself? Like you can't tell which way is up? Life is a confusing basket of emotion and dashed hopes, and when you feel hurt or abandoned, it only gets worse. Do you ever look at your circumstances and think they aren't fair?

I mean, is God even paying attention? Does He realize that you need help? Because you do, right? You don't understand what's happening in your life or why, and you don't know what to do about it.

Sound familiar?

I've lived in five different states, changed zip codes ten times, plus packed and unpacked moving boxes too many times to count. Every move felt a little harder. My heart hurt a little more each time I had to leave. I'd make friends, move away, lose friends, settle in, and start the whole vicious cycle all over again.

Each time, the same questions popped into my mind and heart: Does anyone anywhere really care? Does God care? I'm hurting, trapped in this pit of despair, so where is God?

Regardless what label you give your hurt, it still does the same damage. If it isn't moving and change, maybe it's divorce. Being single. Unemployment. Bankruptcy. Cancer. Fill in the blank.

Everyone experiences brokenness and hurt. It may feel like you're the only person walking around wounded, but you aren't alone. That's why I'm writing this book. I want to encourage you that God sees you and knows when you're hurting. I want to inspire you to experience God's deep, never-ending love for you, no matter what circumstances you're in right now.

You're not alone. You never will be.

But even spiritual wounds can get infected. If you ignore your hurt or only look for a temporary solution, your wounds will fester. It'll take longer to heal. Only God can help us truly bind up the wounds of our past hurts and truly heal our damaged hearts, and though the process isn't easy, great blessings are waiting for you on the other side of your pain.

Why do you think people hide their hurts instead of dealing with them?

_____

What hurts are you hiding today?

_____

Let's take a moment and really dig into the hope-filled chapter of Psalm 139. This amazing passage will help us look into the painful places in our lives that need healing and hope, and we know our Jehovah-Rapha, the God Who Heals, will be right there with us every step of the way.

Psalm 139 is one of the many works of David, king of Israel and the man after God's own heart. Many Bible scholars call this particular psalm the "Crown of the Psalms," mainly because its beautiful language celebrates God's immensity and power alongside His intimate, personal knowledge of each individual in the world. God knows everything. That includes where we are, what we think before we speak, what's in our hearts, and more. There is nothing about us or our lives, private or public, God doesn't know.

Are you scared? Don't be. God doesn't want to scare us. He wants us to understand how powerful He is, that there is nothing we can hide from Him, and that even though He knows all our secrets, He loves us unconditionally and wants to be part of our lives.

It's true. Being aware that God is always watching should motivate us to live holy lives, but performance isn't the point. Pursuing a relationship with Him is.

We have many, many ways to study God's Word, aside from just reading the Bible. One of the most popular—as well as most revealing—methods of study is the Inductive Method. This method has three components: Observation (looking at what it says), Interpretation (thinking through what it means), and Application (taking what the Scripture says and using it in my everyday life).

Let's use the Inductive Bible Study Method to learn more about Psalm 139:1-6.

Psalm 139:1-6 (ESV)
O Lord, you have searched me and known me!
You know when I sit down and when I rise up;
you discern my thoughts from afar.
You search out my path and my lying down
and are acquainted with all my ways.
Even before a word is on my tongue,
behold, O Lord, you know it altogether.

You hem me in, behind and before,
and lay your hand upon me.
Such knowledge is too wonderful for me;
it is high; I cannot attain it.

Observation

In a few sentences, what does this passage say about the attributes of God?

_____

_____

Here are the 3 Big O descriptions of God to hold on to in our biggest times of need:

- **Omniscient:**

God knows all. He has a perfect knowledge of everything. He knows the past, present, and future.
(Isaiah 46:9-10)

- **Omnipotent:**

God possesses all power. He is able to bring into being anything that He has decided to do. (Jeremiah 32:27)

- **Omnipresent:**

God is present everywhere, in all the universe, at all times, in the totality of His character. (Proverbs 15:3)

-from Lord, Heal my Hurts, Kay Arthur, page 278

In your own words, summarize these three attributes of God:
Omniscient:

_____

Omnipotent:

_____

Omnipresent:

_____

Interpretation

What does Psalm 139:5 tell you about the God of hope?

_____

_____

_____

Application

Which of the three Attributes gives you the most comfort?

_____

What hurt or pain are you storing in your heart?

_____

Write and say a short prayer that acknowledges God's attributes and the power of His love to move in your life and heal your hurts.

When I am holding on to my hurts inside, the struggle to maintain my joy is infinitely harder. How about you?

Do you sometimes think you can't go on? Do you feel tired of just existing and going through the motions?

Believe it or not, one of God's prophets felt exactly the same way. His name was Jeremiah, and he wrote two of the books of the Old Testament. This is what he wrote in Jeremiah 8:18 (ESV): **"My joy is gone; grief is upon me; my heart is sick within me."**

Yes, that's in the Bible. Yes, it was said by one of God's prophets. Yes, God knew all about Jeremiah's troubles and his heartaches and his pain, and God never stopped loving him, never abandoned him, and welcomed his lamentations.

In fact, one of Jeremiah's books is called Lamentations. It's the source of many verses that overflow with hope in who God is and how He rescues His children.

Our conversation this week is all about how to get your joy back. We're not going to talk about survival. We're going to talk about how you can thrive and grow and conquer your pain through the power of Jesus Christ, because He's made it possible for us to have hearts that are whole and healed, even after the hurts of life have knocked us down.

Select your favorite verse from Day 1 then flip forward to Day 5 of this chapter and record it in the top box. For the rest of today spend time in prayer meditating and living out the verse you selected.

A Prayer

Dear Holy Spirit, I long to have my joy restored. I'm tired of feeling sad. I know You have a direct connection with God, and I desire to have the same connection with Him. I'm holding on to the scripture that says the joy of the Lord is my strength, but right now I've got very little strength or joy. Help me, Holy Spirit! I want things to change. I know it needs to start with me. I need Your guidance and wisdom to get me through another day. Show me how to live for You. No matter what may come, I will praise Your name, My Rescuer and Redeemer. Amen!

Day 2: God is Faithful

Emilie Barnes: Joy in Spite of Circumstances

Your circumstances determine your future, right?

Nothing is further from the truth. God is the one who determines our rise or fall, and even in the darkest moments of our lives, we can still find Him. No one has more right to speak to this truth than author and speaker Emilie Barnes, who overcame generations of family trauma to become an outspoken force for the hope we have in Jesus Christ.

We're going to spend a little more time than normal with Emilie Barnes because her story is so powerful. Read about her life, her pain, and her hope, and see if you can find yourself in her story.

The story of Emilie's pain began with her grandparents. Her Jewish grandparents lived and worked in Brooklyn, New York, and they had five beautiful children. But after the birth of baby number five, Emilie's grandmother committed suicide. That left Emilie's grandfather with four kids and an infant to raise all by himself. Even though he was a gifted clothes tailor and loved his children, Emilie's grandfather couldn't find a reason to keep living. In his depression and his misery over the loss of his wife, he too committed suicide, only two years after his wife died.

The oldest of the five children, Irene—Emilie Barnes's mother—was left to care for her brothers and sisters. Work was scarce in New York, so Irene packed up her siblings and left for Hollywood, where the jobs were. As a young adult, Irene designed and sewed tennis dresses for celebrities in the 1920s. When she was 29, she met Otto Klein, a 40-year-old Jewish WWI vet who was a chief at Paramount Studios. They married in 1930.

Irene's greatest desire in life was to be a mom. She wanted a family more than anything, but Otto didn't. Twice Irene became pregnant, and twice Otto forced her to have an abortion. Until late in 1933, Irene found herself pregnant a third time but refused to have an abortion. In July 1934, Otto and Irene welcomed their first child, a son, Edmund. Four years later, in April 1938, their daughter Emilie arrived.

For all the noise he made about not wanting a family, Otto loved Emilie. But his relationship with Edmund was rocky from day one. Otto himself was a product of abuse suffered at the hands of his father, so he in turn abused his son. His rage and the memories of the war drove him to alcoholism, and his anger and violence only grew until Irene lived in constant fear of him.

Emilie became the peacekeeper of the home, the only person who could reason with her father.

The summer after Emilie turned 11, her father died. It was something she had hoped for.

But now, Irene had nothing, except hospital bills and debt. Irene's siblings chipped in to help their family stay afloat financially until Irene was able to open a small dress shop in Long Beach. The family lived behind the shop in a three-room apartment, and Irene did everything in her power to make a happy home for her two children.

To this day, Emilie says her mother was a Proverbs 31 woman without even knowing it.

No Real Peace

Her brother, however, held on to his rage and anger, born in him during his childhood years. He kept their home in constant turmoil until he joined the Marine Corps and later married, leaving his mother and sister in peace at last.

At least, peace in the home. But Emilie had no peace in her heart. She had questions about life and death and what happened to people after they were no longer alive. She was confirmed at the Jewish temple at the age of 15, but she didn't find answers there.

Read what the Bible says in Jeremiah 6:14 below:

They offer superficial treatments for my people's mortal wound. They give assurances of peace when there is no peace. (NLT)

What causes you to struggle with peace?

_____

What is the difference between how the world gives peace and how Jesus gives you peace?

_____

The next year, aiming to help her mother sell some dresses, Emilie began attending modeling school, and she befriended the most talented model in her class, a girl named Esther. They spent a week together over the summer break, and one night at the movies, they encountered the Barnes brothers, Bill and Bob. Thanks to Esther, Bob agreed to take Emilie out on a date.

New Introduction and Invitation

Over time, Bob and Emilie fell deeply in love, but Bob told her one day that he couldn't marry her, because she didn't know Jesus. And she didn't. Emilie had never heard of Him. So Bob introduced her. She began going to church with Bob and his family, and one night in her room, Emilie gave her heart to Jesus. She and Bob married a few years later.

They were both young, and they started their family young. So by the time Emilie was 20, they already had one child and another on the way. That's when life turned upside down. Edmund, Emilie's older brother, had become a single parent with three children. But Edmund couldn't care for them, so Bob and Emilie accepted them into their home.

At the age of 21, Emilie Barnes became mother to five children under the age of five.

Holding On To Hope

During this time in Emilie's life, she and her husband never gave up hope for Irene. They continued to hold on to the hope they had in Christ.

Believe in the Lord Jesus, and you will be saved—you and your household. Acts 16:31 (ESV)

Eventually, Emilie's "little Jewish mom" came to Jesus and turned into a fiery, outspoken advocate for Him.

Emilie loved being a mom, but she did look forward to the day when she wouldn't be a mom anymore. At least, she did until that day arrived. When her children left for college, Emilie desperately struggled with her identity and purpose.

New Direction

That's when her mentor, Florence Littauer, told her to write a book. Emilie refused. She wasn't a writer. But Florence wouldn't take no for an answer.

What challenges do you have ahead of you in the near future?

_____

_____

Describe your present mindset as you step out as a risk taker in the coming months.

_____

_____

In 1982, Emilie Barnes signed her first book contract with Harvest House Publishers. Emilie Barnes has published more than 80 books, two of which were written during her struggle with non-Hodgkin's lymphoma—*Safe in the Father's Hands* and *A Cup of Hope.*

The lymphoma eventually led to her death at the age of 78. Emilie had two children, five grandchildren, and three great grandchildren, and she left a legacy of joy that could overcome any adversity. No matter what she faced, no matter how dark the darkness got, Emilie Barnes held on to her joy. And she has helped millions do the same.

Throughout Emilie's story, I can't help but stop and take note of her hurts and the events that should have stolen her hope and joy and hindered her in her life:

- Abusive home
- Father's death
- Hard work in teenage years
- Struggle with no peace
- Married young, mother of five at 21
- Cancer at 50

Yet, Emilie endured. Her faith in the Lord sustained her through the good and bad times of her life. What an inspiration![20]

What are some adjectives you would use to describe Emilie's faith?

_____

How about yourself? What are some adjectives you would use to describe your own faith?

_____

> Take a moment and talk to Jesus about the state of your faith. Wherever you are, Jesus cares. He wants to help you. So write out a prayer and tell Him what you need.

So much of conquering the trials in our life comes down to our perspective. Most folks see a glass of water that is half full or half empty.

Everybody has a different type of glass, depending on who they are or where they come from. Maybe you have a tumbler or a juice glass. Maybe it's an iced tea glass or a mug, a plastic cup, goblet, wine glass, thermos. Maybe yours is brand new. Some may have reached "oldie-but-goodie" status, and others may be cracked and worn out.

Draw your glass below and then, inside, write the adjectives you hope to have as your life-long attributes.

Emilie strived to trust God in the bad times and the good. She saw her glass (no matter how scratched and worn-out it was) half full and ready to be filled. Let's look at a hero in Genesis who had the same attitude and represents a pre-New Testament Jesus lookalike in the Old Testament. His name is Joseph.

Joseph: Trusting God When It Doesn't Make Sense

The Bible doesn't pull punches when it tells stories about the people in its pages. Some stories of biblical heroes don't start out very heroic, and many of them don't end heroically at all. But there is one Bible character who had every reason to turn his back on God—but never did.

This man's name was Joseph, son of Jacob.

> If you remember earlier in this book, we talked about two sisters named Leah and Rachel who were in constant competition with each other. Their father had married them off to the same man, and that man was Jacob. He'd wanted to marry Rachel, but he ended up having to marry Leah too. Leah had many sons, and Jacob didn't really notice, because he didn't love Leah. Rachel, however, Jacob loved, so when she gave birth to a son, Jacob rejoiced. That son was Joseph. You can find this story in Genesis 37-50.

Joseph was his father's favorite son and his brothers' favorite punching bag. In fact, Jacob's obvious favoritism toward Joseph set his brothers against him from the start, and as a young man, Joseph didn't always help the situation.

Joseph had dreams from God, like his father had, but Joseph didn't always know when to keep those dreams to himself. One day, he shared a dream God given him about how his father and his brothers would all bow down to him, that he would be head of their family, even though he was the eleventh son of twelve.

As you can imagine, that didn't make him very popular.

When Joseph was 17, his father sent him to check up on his brothers out in the fields, and when his brothers saw him coming, they grabbed him and threw him into a pit. At first, they intended to leave him to die, but an opportunity arose to sell him into slavery.

And that's exactly what they did.

You can be encouraged because God tells us in Psalm 40:2, "He will lift us up out of the pit." Look up Psalm 40 and write verse 2 in the space provided. Then, double-underline the words *lifted, pit, miry, despair,* and *steadied.*

Talk about unfair. Sure, maybe Joseph had spoken out of line, but he was just a kid. And, yes, Jacob doted on him, but that wasn't Joseph's fault. Joseph didn't deserve his brothers' hate, and being sold into slavery in a foreign land was more than unfair. It was just wrong.

What do you do when someone treats you unfairly?

☐ I long to get even
☐ I get even
☐ I build a wall to keep them out
☐ I tell myself this is God's plan

☐ I become down and depressed
☐ I get super angry
☐ Other

Eventually, Joseph's captors reached Egypt and sold him to a high-ranking officer named Potiphar. Joseph had every reason to fight, to sulk, to give up, but he didn't. Instead, he worked hard, and he found favor with his owner, to the point where Potiphar gave him control over the entire household. Joseph had chosen to trust that God had a plan, no matter how unfair it might seem, and God blessed him for that choice.

Joseph made it his priority to follow God and live obediently no matter what, and it was a good thing, because his troubles were only just beginning.

The Bible tells us that Joseph was a handsome young man, and Potiphar's wife had some dangerous appetites. Potiphar's wife wanted a sexual relationship with Joseph, but Joseph refused her. Repeatedly. Until one day, Potiphar's wife threw herself at him, but Joseph ran away, though not before she took his coat. Spurned and rejected, Potiphar's wife falsely accuses Joseph of rape, and Joseph is thrown into a dungeon.

When Potiphar's wife tempted Joseph into sexual sin, Joseph already knew what his answer would be. He'd set his priorities ahead of time. He knew the attributes and character of God. He knew what would please God and what temptations to avoid. So he didn't have to struggle with the choice. He knew God's Word and God's ways, and he chose to trust God's plan in spite of how much it hurt.

What about you? List a few priorities you have set as a standard for yourself right now that you know are in agreement with God's Word.

_____

_____

_____

What does 1 Peter 2:20 say about enduring for the right priorities? Write the verse in the space provided:

_____

_____

_____

Well, going back to Joseph, I'm not sure we can imagine what he was feeling. Probably not even 20 years old, and Joseph is in the second pit of his life. But even then, he doesn't let his situation get him down.

God gives him favor with the head of the prison, and Joseph even finds himself with some responsibilities while he's a prisoner there. God shows Himself in many ways and opens some pretty miraculous doors for Joseph. Eventually, Joseph is brought out of the prison to interpret a dream for the Pharaoh himself, and as Joseph speaks for God to Pharaoh, everything changes.

Joseph moves from the PIT to the PALACE and becomes the leader of the entire kingdom of Egypt. Talk about an upgrade.

We know the story of Joseph, so it's clear to us that God's fingerprints are all over this narrative. God guided Joseph every step of the way, but by that same token, Joseph chose to be obedient too.

How do you think God guides you through your tough circumstances?

- ☐ Through prayer
- ☐ Through God's Word
- ☐ Through dreams
- ☐ Through circumstances
- ☐ Through others

Now don't wander off, because the story isn't over yet. And God still has a big surprise up His sleeve. Up in the land of Canaan where Joseph's family lives, they're experiencing a horrible famine. So Joseph's brothers make the long journey to Egypt to buy food, which is where Joseph's childhood dream is finally fulfilled. His brothers bow down to him, although they don't recognize him.

Joseph could have sought revenge. He could have had them killed or thrown in a pit just like they had done to him. He could have publicly humiliated them. He could have done any number of things to hurt them, and not one person who knew his story would have held it against him.

But Joseph didn't think that way. In Joseph's perspective, God had the whole situation under control from the beginning.

Check out his words to his brothers in Genesis 50:20 (NLT).

"You intended to harm me, but God intended it all for good. He brought me to this position so I could save the lives of many people."

Joseph had the power to kill or imprison his brothers, who had wronged him unfairly so many years ago, but instead he chose to be obedient and forgive them. Because of that choice, Joseph saved his family, and he has provided a template for us to follow when we face life circumstances that don't seem fair.

C.S. Lewis called pain God's megaphone. We can see this truth in Joseph's story. Whenever Joseph was in the pit, hurting and feeling alone, God was shouting to him. And it was Joseph's choices during those times of hurting and darkness that have been a blessing to our world.

In your pain, what is God shouting to you?

_____

God tells us in His Word that He is all-powerful, all-present, and all-knowing (remember the three Big O's from earlier?), and that means nothing happens without His knowledge and permission. God is truly in control.

Look up 2 Corinthians 1:8-9. What does Paul say happened to him in this passage? And why?

_____

_____

What did Paul do as a result? And why?

_____

_____

Now is the time, and today is the day to choose to be a Joseph. You can decide to follow God no matter what before you face difficult circumstances, just like Joseph did. Write a statement of commitment in the space provided to help you be the Joseph you need to be.

_____

_____

Select your favorite verse from Day 2 then flip forward to Day 5 of this chapter and record it in the top box. For the rest of today spend time in prayer meditating and living out the verse you selected.

A Prayer

Lord, I believe You are Faithful and in control, but I'm in and out of the pit of despair and looking for Your hand to rescue me. I know You are able as King of kings and Lord of lords to pull me out of the pit and set me on solid ground. Help me, Lord! Speak to my heart. I am listening. I want to be more like Joseph and live my life only for Your glory. Amen!

Day 3: In God We Trust

Just before one of my family's big moves, my children and I learned a valuable lesson about sadness and tears. We were moving from Pennsylvania to upstate New York, and our church family had invited all of us—my kids, my husband, and I—to stand at the front of the sanctuary for prayer. As we stood there with our church family around us, embraced by their arms, surrounded by their love, our hearts were so touched. As they prayed for us, we couldn't stop the tears.

Our pastor prayed for each one of my children by name, speaking words of power over them. I can almost hear his voice again as I write this. "Kids, never be ashamed to cry. It's okay to weep. Tears from God. He holds them in His bottle. Jesus himself wept."

Wow!

My kids gained a new perspective on letting your emotions show and being real with God. It's joyous to know we can experience freedom in our tears when we know the truth. After all, the Bible tells us in John 11:35, "Jesus wept."

Open your Bible and read Psalm 56.
In the blank provided, write a verse from this Psalm that stands out to you:

_____

_____

Why is that verse important to you right now?

_____

_____

> Using the verse you identified from Psalm 56, write a prayer to God. Tell Jesus what's happening in your life right now and ask Him to provide a rescue or an answer.

I want to focus on verse 8 for a moment.

You have kept count of my tossings; put my tears in your bottle. Are they not in your book? Psalm 56:8

When we are hurting, sometimes we can cry and cry and cry. Over the years, as you've dealt with real brokenness in your life and in the world, would your tears fill a glass? A pitcher? A swimming pool?

"The fact that Jesus came to earth where he suffered and died does not remove pain from our lives. But it does show that God did not sit idly by and watch us suffer in isolation. He became one of us. Thus, in Jesus, God gives us an up-close and personal look at his response to human suffering. All our questions about God and suffering should, in fact, be filtered through what we know about Jesus." - Philip Yancey, *Where Is God When It Hurts?*

Where is God during all that sadness? When we're crying our eyes out, does He even notice? The answer is yes. He is right beside us, walking every step of the way with us, and according to Scripture He catches our tears in His bottle.

I didn't think much about keeping tears in a bottle until I realized it might have been a historical practice. Though some sources disagree, many people believe that tear bottles were used in eras dating back to the Roman Empire.

Lachrymatory bottles, or tear bottles, may have been used as early as the Roman Era to catch and contain the tears of mourners. Legend has it that mourners were paid to cry into these vessels, so the more they cried, the more they got paid. Tear bottles grew in popularity during the Victorian Era, when widows would collect their tears and allow them to evaporate as an indication of their period of mourning. Reportedly, tears bottles were also used during the Civil War in America. Women supposedly collected their tears and saved them until their husbands returned from battle as a sign of how much they were missed.

In truth, most archaeologists don't believe tear bottles were actually used to collect tears. In most instances, the residue found inside tear bottles has been perfume or ointments. But regardless if it were something historical people did or not, the Bible tells us it's something God does.

God has a tear bottle, where He catches and collects every one of our sorrows. We can know He cares about our cares, and eventually the day will come when we have no more need for tear bottles—because God will wipe the tears from our eyes. What a beautiful picture of grace and mercy from our loving God!

Look up and fill in the blanks for the following verses as inspiration as you grow through your hurt and pain.

Deuteronomy 31:6 – He will _____ _____ you nor _____ you.

Psalm 80:7 – _____ us, God Almighty; _____ _____ face shine _____ _____.

Psalm 107:20 – He sent _____ _____ _____ and _____ them; he rescued them.

Psalm 126:5-6 – Those who _____ _____ _____
will reap with _____ _____ joy.

Revelation 21:4 – He will _____ _____ _____
from their _____.

No matter what you are facing, never forget your story isn't over yet.

Select your favorite verse from Day 3 then flip forward to Day 5 of this chapter and record it in the top box. For the rest of today spend time in prayer meditating and living out the verse you selected.

In Psalm 56:3, David declares to God, "When I am afraid, I will put my trust in you." Coming from someone like David who faced tremendous danger and struggles in his life, this statement means a lot. And since we serve the same God David did, we can tell God the same thing when we're scared.

Remind yourself today of who is in control of your life. Say this out loud:

"I trust God. He's got this."

Life won't always make sense, but you can trust that God knows what He's doing. So you don't have to be afraid.

A Prayer

Heavenly Father, I've cried so many nights I must have filled a bucket, not a bottle. How long, Lord, will these worries and fears be a struggle in my life? Forgive me for trying to do life alone. I'm impatient and anxious. I know You are in control, but I continue to try to take over. Today I surrender my will and family over to You. I give You complete permission to take it all, and I will follow wherever You lead. Help me follow You with all my heart and soul. Amen!

Day 4: What to Say to Yourself

The next time your friend makes a mistake, tell them they're a loser. Tell them they don't deserve anything good in their lives, and that they'll never amount to anything.

Have I got your attention? Good, because you should never say anything like that to someone you know, especially not someone you love. Everybody knows that, and if you spoke that way to another person, people would blacklist you as being cruel or mean.

So why do you and I talk to ourselves that way?

If it's not okay to speak those cruel things to people around you, it's not okay to speak such things to yourself.

"Control your inner dialogue. Talk to yourself positively all the time." – Brian Tracy

Your words are powerful, whether you're speaking to yourself or someone else. Words can inspire or depress, encourage or discourage, build up or tear down. Words can be one of our greatest tools, but also one of our most damaging weapons when used against each other and our own selves.

The book of Proverbs is full of wisdom for how to speak and how not to speak too. You'd be hard-pressed to find a chapter in Proverbs that doesn't address wisdom or foolishness or how we're supposed to treat each other.

Words Have Power. *Look up the verse and fill in the blanks.*
Proverbs 10:19

Proverbs 11:12

Proverbs 13:3

Proverbs 15:1

Proverbs 16:24

Proverbs 18:13

Proverbs 19:14

Proverbs 21:23

Proverbs 29:11

Proverbs 29:20

What do you say to yourself when you wake up? What about when you see yourself in the mirror? Or when you're running late? Or when someone criticizes you?

Are your words cruel? Is what you're saying to yourself true? Is it something God would say to you, His precious child?

If it isn't, you shouldn't say it. Not even to yourself.

> **"Even though I'd like to avoid the circumstance or situation, I will not. Avoidance behavior will only increase my anxiety. I will go ahead, experience the unpleasant feelings, and I'll get through it."**
> **- William Backus**

> Stop and ask Jesus to reveal to you the truth about yourself and how He feels about you. Give yourself permission to experience His unconditional love and stop being so hard on yourself.

Our lives are full of hurt and brokenness, and no one understands it like Jesus. He lived in our broken world. He felt the same hurt and pain we do. He experienced all the same emotions and traumas and discouraging moments that have poked holes in our dreams. So He understands what we're going through.

Do you think Jesus ever thought cruel things about Himself?

When you get stuck in the vicious cycle of discouragement and depression, it's easy to feel trapped, and when you feel trapped, sometimes you need someone to pin blame on. If you know your position is a result of your own choices, it makes sense to blame yourself. And don't get me wrong, accepting responsibility is right and good, but if you cross the line into self-hatred and self-loathing, you're not honoring God with your speech.

So how are we supposed to talk to ourselves? What are we supposed to say when we get stuck in the repetitive cycle of hurt and pain, and the only person we can take out our frustrations on is ourselves?

Talk to God about it. Take your hurt and your pain to the Lord. Tell Him what you're feeling, and let Him reassure you. Let Him calm your fears. Let Him soothe your soul.

He will.

It's what He does.

What To Say To God

Instead of hating on yourself when you're hurting and frustrated, here are four prayers:

1. *Dear God, I don't understand. Help me trust You.*

This can be a tough one. After all, nobody wants to admit they don't understand. None of us want to be the person who needs a crutch, but God isn't offering a crutch at all. A crutch assumes that you'll still be carrying part of your own weight. God wants to take all our weight, even the parts we don't want to give Him.

Read Proverbs 3:5-6 below.

> **Trust in the Lord** with all your heart, **and do not lean on your own understanding. In all your ways acknowledge him, and he will make straight your paths. (ESV)**

This is a verse you should memorize. Write it on an index card if nothing else. Carry it with you everywhere you go, because this concept will change your life.

This is one of God's promises. Trust Him with everything you have, and don't try to make life make sense on your own terms. Believe that your life is about God, and He'll show you what path you're supposed to take.

Write a few sentences about something God is doing in your life that you are struggling to understand.

_____

_____

What would change if you were willing to trust God to work the situation out instead of trying to understand what He's doing?

_____

_____

It's okay if you don't understand what's happening in your life right now. You don't need to, because God does. All you have to do is trust Him.

> **"My thoughts are nothing like your thoughts," says the Lord. "And my ways are far beyond anything you could imagine. For just as the heavens are higher than the earth, so my ways are higher than your ways, and my thoughts higher than your thoughts." Isaiah 55:8-9 (NLT)**

2. Dear God, I need Your help. I need Your love.

Sometimes the hurt and pain in our lives runs so deeply that we can't even express it in words. Sometimes all we can do is just cry for help and ask God to love us.

You have nothing to fear. He does. Intensely. He loves you so much that you can't even imagine it, and nothing you do or fail to do will change how much He loves you.

Read Psalm 109:26 below:

> **Help me, O Lord my God! Save me according to your steadfast love! (ESV)**

If you describe a characteristic or person as steadfast, what are you saying?

_____

If you could believe God's love is steadfast, how would that change your life? Your relationship with Him?

_____

Memorize Psalm 109:26 and use it as a rallying cry the next time you feel so hurt that you can't take another step. God's steadfast love is waiting to wrap you up in a warm embrace.

Be encouraged! Even if you can't find the words to pray, God sees your tears. He knows your heart. Your cries travel to God even when you can't speak them out loud.

3. Dear God, I can't do life alone. Please send me Your divinely selected person to help me get through this hurt and pain.

American Christians are all about freedom. We are free and have been made free and should make the most of our freedom. So that means we have to do everything ourselves. We have to work harder, pray longer, sing louder, and bounce back faster than anyone else, and we have convinced ourselves that we can do it on our own.

It's a lie.

None of us can do life alone, especially if we've been hurt or torn or broken. We think we need to hide our scars, but hiding and ignoring them only delays the inevitable breakdown. We have to face our hurt and our pain, and we don't have to do it by ourselves.

Read and memorize John 14:16.

And I will ask the Father, and he will give you another Helper, to be with you forever. (ESV)

If you know Jesus, you have the Holy Spirit, and you'll never be alone. God lives inside you, praying for you, encouraging you, supporting you in everything you face. But not just the Holy Spirit is on your side.

You are surrounded by other believers who are struggling through life as much as you are. The honest truth is that concealing our wounds from each other only does more damage. God allows us to experience hurt and pain in our lives for many different reasons, but one of the greatest blessings of our scars is how God can redeem them.

That horrible pain you experienced can become something beautiful that will bless and encourage someone else. But not if you hide it.

No more hiding. You never know how God might use your story to help another person.

4. Dear God, I know You promise to never leave me. Please reveal Yourself to me in a mighty way.
When you don't know what to do, go back to basics. Go back to what you know for sure. God has told us over and over again that He will never leave us, He will never forsake us, and that He will always be by our side.

Sometimes, all you need to do to help the hurting is to say what you know is true.

Read and memorize Romans 8:38.

I am convinced that nothing can ever separate us from God's love. Neither death nor life, nor angels nor demons, neither our fears for today nor our worries about tomorrow—not even the powers of hell can separate us from God's love. (NLT)

God's love will follow you wherever you go. Nothing can ever separate Him from you, and if you can't see Him, it isn't because He's gone away. It's because you aren't listening.

So stop what you're doing. Be calm. Open your heart to God's Word, to His voice, and let Him speak to You. You may not always like what He has to say, but you can trust that whatever He tells you is true.

By talking to yourself about the things you have to be grateful for, you can fill your mind with thoughts that soar and sing. – Dale Carnegie

Select your favorite verse from Day 4 then flip forward to Day 5 of this chapter and record it in the top box. For the rest of today spend time in prayer meditating and living out the verse you selected.

A Prayer

Dear Jesus, help me begin a new way of talking to myself. I desire to speak and live Your truth as a wise person and not a fool. I believe You will reveal to me why I don't respect myself. I want to honor You with my mouth toward others and myself. When I feel hopeless, remind me of Your scriptures that tell me there is eternal hope in God. I love the peace I have when I spend time with You in prayer. Keep me in Your love as I lean on Your provision and protection each day. Amen!

Day 5: Talking with God

As you complete each daily section of this study, write down your favorite verse from each day.

Day 1: _____

Day 2: _____

Day 3: _____

Day 4: _____

God never stops speaking to us, whether through the Holy Spirit or worship songs, through the words of a good friend or the beauty of a morning sunrise. You can find God wherever you go, whatever you do. He's there, listening, ready to start the day at your side.

You want to have a real conversation with God? The first step is to read the Bible.

Devotionals are good. Bible studies are excellent. But reading the Bible yourself is essential to your relationship with God.

Bible reading is a sure way to hear God's voice, because the Bible is God's Word, and it's uniquely, specifically in tune with your individual needs through the power of the Holy Spirit.

If you've hit a difficult place in life, here are a few suggested verses to read. Look them up. Read them. Memorize them. Write them on a card or text them to yourself. Read one every day and let the truth sink into your heart as you live your life.

Psalm 88	1 Corinthians 6:20
Psalm 86	2 Corinthians 5:15
Romans 5:6-8	Galatians 5:6
1 John 4:9-10	Romans 5:3
Hebrews 11-12	James 1:2-4
Matthew 22:37-39	

Journal the Journey:

1. Write a few destructive thoughts you say to yourself on a regular basis.
2. Now write three truths from God's Word to counter those destructive thoughts you have been saying to yourself. For help with references, turn back to Day 3 or Day 4 in this chapter.
3. Write 10 statements of truth in your journal about God and His love for you during the difficult times of life. For additional encouragement, you can include a Bible verse after each statement.

A Prayer

Oh, God, I love You. I'm learning how amazing life can be with You as my eternal hope. Help me to be consistent in meeting with you every day and reading Your Word. Thank You for answering my prayer and showing up in ways I couldn't even imagine. I want to live a hope-filled life that brings You Glory. Help me not to stumble following the hopeless message of the world. I'm yours, Lord. Everything I've got is Yours, Lord. My confidence is in You, and my hope is sure. Love you, Lord. Amen!

Mentoring Tip: Mentoring relationships change lives by meeting on a weekly basis to be encouraged and reminded of the hope we have in Christ.

CONVERSATION 8

Does God Really Have
a Plan for Me?

*God, your God, has blessed you in everything you have
done. He has guarded you in your travels through this
immense wilderness. For forty years now, God, your God,
has been right here with you. You haven't lacked one thing.*
Deuteronomy 2:7 (MSG)

Day 1: God is WITH You

When I was a little girl, I used to mix my words up. My parents told me
stories about the crazy things I would say. They thought it was adorable,
but I'm pretty sure they were biased.

My dad's favorite thing that I would say came whenever he and my
mom were leaving the house for a date or other event. I had to stay behind,
and I would trail along after them exclaiming, "Don't go out with me!"

Of course, what I meant was: "Don't go without me!" But in my little
girl mind, I'd jumbled the words all around. They were the right words,
but they were in the wrong order.

My dad thought it was wonderful, and he'd always tease me about it.
"Jayme Lee," he'd say, "you just keep saying that, especially to all the boys
you meet."

That little four-letter preposition *with* is really important in our lives, and it's also really important in the Bible. How do I know that? Well, when God uses a word or phrase more than once in Scripture, that's usually means we are supposed to pay attention.

Do you know how many times the word *with* appears in the Bible? **More than 2,000 times.**

Are you paying attention yet? I sure am.

God constantly reminds His people that He is with them all throughout Scripture, both in the Old Testament and the New Testament. God promises that He will be with His people—*with you*—more than 1,600 times.

God is trying to communicate something to us. Don't you think?

So what does it mean for God to be with us? How does that even work? How are we supposed to live our lives with God?

It's a good thing the Israelites had those very same questions, so we can see what they did and how they accepted a relationship with God that He made possible.

Look up and read Deuteronomy 5:1-5.

This amazing passage in the Bible chronicles a moment when Moses is reminding the Israelites that they are not now (nor have they ever been) alone. God had been with them every step of the way.

This passage is also written below. Grab your highlighter and mark every time you see the phrases *with us* and *with you*.

And Moses summoned all Israel and said to them, "Hear, O Israel, the statutes and the rules that I speak in your hearing today, and you shall learn them and be careful to do them. The Lord our God made a covenant with us in Horeb. Not with our fathers did the Lord make this covenant, but with us, who are all of us here alive today. The Lord spoke with you face to face at the mountain, out of the midst of the fire, while I stood between the Lord and you at that time, to declare to you the word of the Lord. For you were afraid because of the fire, and you did not go up into the mountain. (Deuteronomy 5:1-5 ESV)

Are you encouraged? You should be. God is with you too!

> **"When you realize God's purpose for your life isn't just about you, He will use you in a mighty way." - Tony Evans**

Think about Noah. Noah is one of those Bible characters that just about everyone is familiar with, even if you've never read the Bible. Everybody knows that Noah built the ark, but do you know how long it took Noah to build that giant boat?

It took him 120 years.

120 years!

Granted, people lived longer back in those days, but that's half the age of the United States! That's a long time! Put yourself in Noah's sandals if you think that was an easy job. He must have been nervous and questioning nearly every moment of those 120 years.

Sure, maybe when he first started work on the Ark, he was confident. He was positive. He had a job to do, and he was going to do it to the best of his ability. But as the weeks and months and years went by, he had to have experienced doubt.

How did he keep going? Well, let's read exactly what God said to him in the following verses from the Book of Genesis.

Genesis 6:18.
But I will establish my covenant with you, and you shall come into the ark, you, your sons, your wife, and your sons' wives with you.

Genesis 9:12
And God said, "This is the sign of the covenant that I make between me and you and every living creature that is with you, for all future generations."

Grab your highlighter again. In the verses above, highlight every instance of *with you* or *you*. Now count them up. How many times did God say *with you* or *you/your* in those two verses alone? _____

Those aren't just casual statements either. Those are promises, not just to Noah individually but to all of Noah's family, his future descendants, and for all future generations. And God always keeps His promises.

Let's do some digging!

Grab your Bible and look up the following verses. Write them out in the spaces provided and then highlight every time you see the phrase *with you*.

Genesis 26:24

_____

_____

_____

Amos 5:14

_____

_____

_____

2 Corinthians 1:21

_____

_____

_____

God desires a relationship with you. He made you. He loves you. Do you understand that? Even if you can't understand that kind of love, can you accept it?

It doesn't matter where you come from. It doesn't matter who your parents are. It doesn't matter how well you've raised your kids or how many times you've forgiven people who've hurt you. It doesn't even matter if you've read your Bible today.

None of those things will keep God from desiring to spend time with you.

In Christian circles, we talk about having a relationship with God, but do we really grasp what it means to experience every day side by side with Him? Living your life with God will revolutionize everything about you and your life and how you connect with those around you.

Maybe you're wondering why God would want to spend time with you. I can understand that thought. When we know how awesome and wonderful God is, the thought of Him desperately seeking an intimate friendship with us is overwhelming. Laughable, even.

But try to see it from God's point of view. When we have given our lives to Jesus, God sees us—the real us. Not the failures. Not the flaws. Not the well-intentioned disasters we always seem to get caught up in. He sees us as He created us to be, and He sees our potential to do great and mighty things with His strength. He wants to help us, to transform us from where we are to where He created us to be.

Each one of us has a purpose. God made us with a specific plan in mind, and if we want to achieve that purpose, we have to accept God's strength and direction. Because we can't achieve God's purposes without God in our lives.

Nobody can.

> Write out and say a prayer to God thanking Him for His unconditional, unchanging love.

Not long after God sent Moses to rescue the Israelites from Egypt (the ten plagues, the parting of the Red Sea, "Let my people go!" and so on and so forth), this slave nation of millions ended up wandering around in a desert wilderness. Not for a month. Not for ten years. **For forty years.**

They had to wander as punishment because they had forgotten God's promise. What was His promise?

That He'd always be with them.

So to punish the generation that had forgotten, God let the Israelites wander in the Sinai wilderness until they perished, leaving their children behind. Those children had grown up in the wilderness, but they grew up witnessing miracles and understanding very clearly that even though their parents had doubted God, God had never left them. God was still with them to that very day.

By the way, are you picking up the pattern here? Noah spent 120 years building a boat. Moses and the complaining children of Israel wandered in a desert for 40 years. Even Jesus had to wait 30 years before He did His first miracle. Even after God has called us to do something, we still have to trust Him on the timing.

Take a moment and imagine you're going on a camping trip. Let's make this an epic adventure too. Let's say that you're going to be traveling for 40 days. You're going to be sleeping outside, cooking over a campfire, enjoying God's creation all around you. Maybe you'll drive into the mountains—the Rockies or the Appalachians. You're going to hike and boat and fish and marvel at everything God has made.

With all that in mind, think about the Israelites. Technically they were camping. And not for 40 days—40 years! And there weren't just a few of them. It wasn't just one family out on an adventure in the mountains. It was millions of people, lost in a barren desert wasteland.

There weren't any camping supplies. No outdoorsman outlets. No pop-up tents. No grocery stores. When their shoes and clothing wore out, they couldn't buy more. When their food ran low, they couldn't just pop into a Chick-Fil-A for a chicken sandwich and a sweet tea.

With all that in mind, we opened this day with Deuteronomy 2:7. Rewrite it in the space below:

_____

_____

_____

Focus on that last sentence. Write it again here:

_____

_____

_____

Not one thing. The Israelites had everything they needed. Now, they probably didn't have everything they wanted. That's an important distinction. But God provided for their needs on an hourly basis. He remained faithful to them in a supernatural way when they had given (and continued for forty years to give) Him every reason to give up on them.

He never did. He still hasn't. And He won't ever.

The same is true for you.

Before and After
Most of us will all have to spend time in a wilderness of some sort before God reveals His plans for us. Not everyone's wilderness will look the same, but just know that a wilderness doesn't mean God has abandoned

you. Once God says He's with you, nothing can change that, and once you conquer your wilderness, God will take you to the next level in your walk with Him.

Let's look at some examples from the Bible of how God used a wilderness experience to take His people to another level in their journey with Him.

MOSES (Exodus 3 – Deuteronomy 34)

Before God's Miracles – Moses was an outcast, a shepherd hiding from his past and his future. He'd fled Egypt because he'd broken the law, and he had no intention of ever going back again.

After God's Miracles – Moses led the entire nation of Israel out of slavery in Egypt, and over a period of 40+ years, he guided them through the wilderness as God's chosen leader. Even secular scholars regard Moses as the greatest leader in history.

While he was in his wilderness, Moses felt he would struggle with being the mouthpiece of God. Can you blame him? He begged God to allow him a helper, and God responded with Moses's brother, Aaron. On one hand, that was great. On the other hand, Moses' fear and insecurity about what God could or couldn't do prevented him from experiencing God's best plan for his life.

How about you? When it comes to talking, what do you struggle with the most? Check the box that describes where you are at today.

- ☐ Talking to anyone about God
- ☐ Talking to God
- ☐ One-on-one conversations
- ☐ In public
- ☐ Talk too much

DAVID (1 Samuel 15 – 2 Samuel)

Before Becoming King – David was just a kid, and he'd done incredible things for his country. But the current king of Israel—Saul—wanted to kill him. David spent years running for his life.

After Becoming King – David is known as the greatest king to rule Israel. He's called a man after God's own heart. He leads his nation to victory after victory and sets the stage for the most prosperous era Israel ever knew.

David ended up in a wilderness while he had a close relationship with God. It wasn't that David had stopped doing what God said was right and then he ended up in a wilderness. No. David kept on doing what was right, and he found himself in a wilderness anyway. But sometimes God uses the wildernesses in our lives to teach us important lessons about ourselves.

What do you think David learned from waiting in the wilderness while he hid from Saul?

_____

_____

What are you waiting on right now?

_____

_____

What are you doing while you are living in this waiting period?

_____

_____

> **JOSEPH** (Genesis 30 – 50)
>
> *Before His Dream Was Fulfilled* – Joseph had everything. He was his father's favorite. He had a life full of potential as one of the twelve sons of Jacob. But then, his brothers sell him into slavery, and he lives in captivity in Egypt for more than 12 years while he endures the assassination of his character and the pain of being rejected and forgotten.
>
> *After His Dream Was Fulfilled* – In a single day, Joseph goes from the filthy rags of a prison to the glorious throne room of a palace. He becomes the most powerful man in the entire world after Pharaoh himself, and he holds the key to the world's food supply during a devastating famine.

If you think your family has trouble, let me introduce you to Jacob's 12 sons. Talk about dysfunctional. Joseph hadn't really done much of anything to deserve his brothers' hatred, but they hated him anyway.

What part of the rejection Joseph experienced from his brothers can you relate to?

_____

Are you waiting for God to promote you or move you to the next level in life? If you are, how are you preparing now for what God will do with you tomorrow?

_____

Select your favorite verse from Day 1 then flip forward to Day 5 of this chapter and record it in the top box. For the rest of today spend time in prayer meditating and living out the verse you selected.

A Prayer

Dear Lord, thank You for Your unconditional and overflowing love for me. Please show me today in everything I do and experience that You are with me. I can't trust my feelings. I

feel alone, but You tell me I'm not. I'm calling out to You. Be
with me, Lord Jesus. I confess I'm weak and weary, but I long
to be strong and confident. Move in my life in a mighty way
and lead me to Your will and purpose for my life. Thank You
for constantly wanting to be with me in the deepest parts of
my life. I love you, Lord. Amen!

Day 2: You Have a Purpose

Joni Eareckson Tada: God's Plan Is Bigger Than Me

We've all been 17 before, with the most exciting moments of our lives out
in front of us. You're full of potential. You've got your entire future ahead
of you, and you're bulletproof. So when 17-year-old Joni Eareckson ended
up in a wheelchair after a diving accident, you can imagine her despair.

Her dreams, her life's purpose, everything she'd ever wanted vanished
in that moment in 1967 when she lost the use of her legs and arms. She
hated her paralysis so much that she took her frustration out on her
wheelchairs, driving them into walls so they would break. She drowned
her sorrows in alcohol and waited to die.[21]

But God wasn't done with her. From her perspective, her life's purpose
had been destroyed, but from God's perspective, her purpose was only just
beginning.

God's grace through loving friends and studying the Bible, drew Joni
out of her depression and despair, and after two years of rehabilitation, she
could see the world with new eyes. She had a new dream, a passion to help
others who had suffered like she had.

Joni Eareckson Tada is now the Founder and CEO of Joni and Friends
International Disability Center where she serves as an advocate for the
disabled. Over long months in rehabilitation, she taught herself to paint
with a brush clenched between her teeth, and now her works of art are
highly sought after and even collected.[22]

She didn't stop with painting. She writes books too. Her memoir *The
God I Love* released in 2003. Her book *A Place of Healing* hit the shelves in
2011. After a struggle with breast cancer, she wrote *Diagnosed with Breast
Cancer: Life after Shock*, which released in 2012.

Joni has written and released multiple books on healing and walking with God through trials and difficult situations. In October 2016, she released a title that won best devotional book in the ECPA's 2017 Christian Book Awards, *A Spectacle of Glory*.

> **"There are more important things in life than walking and having the use of your hands. It sounds incredible, but I really would rather be in this wheelchair knowing Jesus as I do than be on my feet without Him."**
> **– Joni Eareckson Tada**

If you had asked Joni about her life's purpose when she was 17, she wouldn't have had an answer for you. She would have told you that her life was over, that she couldn't accomplish anything anymore.

If you had asked God why He took away Joni's purpose in life, what do you think He would have said?

Try asking her about her life's purpose now. On July 30, 2017, Joni celebrated the 50th anniversary of her paralysis, and she has made the most of every moment, choosing to pursue God's purpose for her life instead of mourning the opportunities she lost. She's doing more for God's kingdom today than most people who aren't confined to a wheelchair.

If you're facing an uncertain future right now, what pressures in your life are adding to your despair?

_____

_____

> Take a moment and bring your fears and concerns to Jesus. The list of pressures you just wrote? Read them off to Jesus right now. Entrust your fears and concerns to Him and see what He does.

Think back to Conversation 7, specifically on Day 2. This was the day we talked about Joseph, the young man who was sold in to slavery, treated unfairly, forgotten, and left to rot in prison.

Joseph's circumstances weren't fair at all. They were extreme, like losing your mobility at 17. Joseph could have become bitter. He could have allowed resentment to taint his beliefs about God and God's purposes for his life. But he didn't.

And years later, when he was given the chance to take revenge on the people who'd hurt him the most, what did he say?

"You intended to harm me, but God intended it all for good. He brought me to this position so I could save the lives of many people." **(Genesis 50:20)**

I like that word, *intended*. God is full of intention. He has purposes, plans, targets, and goals for all of His children, and nothing can stop them. Even as Joseph's brothers plotted to destroy Joseph, God was a giant step ahead of them. God had already figured out how to use their evil intentions to not only save Joseph's entire family from starvation—but also the rest of the world too! What a great God!

Joseph didn't know any of this, but God had planned it from the beginning. Before Joseph was even born, God already knew what was going to happen to him. So Joseph's struggles didn't catch God unaware. God had already masterminded a happy ending for Joseph's story before Joseph even existed.

Before Joni Eareckson Tada was born, God knew about the devastating injury that would take away her physical freedom. He knew the pain and despair and sorrow she would feel, and He didn't let her suffer alone. He was with her every step of the way, gently calling to her, kindly whispering to her that she hadn't lost her purpose. She was just discovering it.

God isn't a sweep-up boy who follows along after you with a dustpan and a brush, fretting over the messes you've made and struggling to piece together your life in a divine pattern that makes sense. He doesn't put on a hazmat suit so an evil situation won't contaminate His holy reputation. Our God gets His hands dirty. He's right down in the middle of our mess alongside us, walking with us every step of the way, holding our hand and cheering us on.

Reflecting on past disappointments, do you think any of those things surprised the God of the universe?

Take comfort in knowing that God hasn't removed His hands from the wheel of your life for one nanosecond. Everything that has happened in your life—the good, the bad, the joyful, the painful—is playing a role in shaping your character so that you can do what God created you to do according to the purpose He has for you.

Write down a difficult situation you're facing today.

_____

_____

Have you learned anything about God and your relationship with Him as you live through this difficult situation?

_____

_____

What is keeping you from deepening and strengthening your relationship with God? Is it how you look? Is it where you were born? Do you really think any of those things matter to the God who hand-made every inch of you?

_____

_____

Your trials and struggles and difficult circumstances are more than just random bad luck. The tough stuff of life has more meaning than you realize. Your problems have a purpose.

Look up Job 42:2 in the English Standard Version and write it out for encouragement.

_____

_____

You have the power to choose how you see your problems. Joni Eareckson Tada chose to see her circumstances as an opportunity to achieve a purpose bigger than herself. You can do the same thing.

Only God knows what He will do with your difficult situation. Only He can tell whose life He'll use your story to transform. But no matter what you're going through, you can trust that God has a plan, and He knows what He's doing.

Even if people in your life intend harm toward you, God intends only good, and He is big enough to use any situation in your life for good.

God is the only Person in the universe Who can take something bad and transform it into something wonderful and truly good.

Rahab: A Scarlet Thread of Faith

My grandkids can play *I Spy* for hours. Hours and hours. How many ways can you describe the candy bars in the grocery store checkout line? I'm sure my grandkids have set a record. They love figuring out the clues and discovering the secret first so they can win the game.

Spying games are fun for kids (and grown-ups) to play, but there were a couple of spies in the Bible who weren't playing. They got themselves into a lot of trouble, and they had to ask for help from someone they never expected—a woman named Rahab.

It's not unusual that God's people would seek help from a woman. The Old Testament has many stories of women who accomplished heroic deeds in God's name. What is unusual about this situation, however, is that Rahab wasn't just a woman. She was a prostitute.

You can find her story in Joshua 2.

The Book of Joshua takes place after the Israelites have finished wandering in the wilderness for 40 years. Moses has died, and the leadership of the nation of Israel has passed to Joshua.

We first met Joshua when he and eleven other spies went to snoop on the Promised Land after the Israelites crossed the Red Sea. Joshua and his buddy Caleb both believed that with God's power, they could conquer the Promised Land; the other ten disagreed and convinced the rest of the people to disagree too. That's how they ended up wandering in the wilderness until that whole generation died—except for Joshua and Caleb.

So as the children of Israel are poised to enter Canaan, the land that God promised to them, Joshua takes the reins of his people. But there are a couple of really big obstacles for Joshua to overcome—namely a city called Jericho.

Rahab lived in Jericho, a city in Canaan that was widely considered to be impenetrable. Archaeologists have determined that the walls of the city of Jericho were 20 feet high and 8 feet wide, and Rahab lived in the walls. Her home was actually built into them.

No beautiful palaces or downtown apartments for Rahab. Nobody wanted her as their neighbor, not even in a wicked city like Jericho. She is set apart at the beginning of her life by her own community because of her lifestyle.

Can you imagine how lonely her life had to be? Rahab wouldn't have experienced any close relationships. She wouldn't have been able to take true satisfaction in her career. It was all she could do to make ends meet, and the only way she could do that was to allow herself to be used and treated like an object.

Her own people would have viewed her as less than human. She was a thing to be traded and sold, used for pleasure and then discarded.

What kind of purpose could a woman like that have in God's plan?

Read Joshua 2:1-8.

So, what exactly is happening here? Joshua sent two spies ahead of the whole army to get the lay of the land and see if Jericho was really as impenetrable as the rumors said. The spies got in all right, but once they were in, somebody blew their cover.

And who do you think gave them shelter?

Rahab.

The King of Jericho, his whole army, they were all searching for these two spies. They even came to Rahab's house and demanded that she turn over the men.

This was Rahab's defining moment. She could have told the soldiers where the Israelite spies were hiding. She had concealed them on her own roof. She knew exactly where they were. And maybe, just maybe, her own community might have accepted her. If she had demonstrated that she was one of them in spite of the fact that she was a prostitute, maybe they would have thought better of her.

But that's not what Rahab did. She told the soldiers that the men had already left and that she didn't know where they had gone. So the soldiers went off on a wild goose chase, and Rahab helped the Israelite spies escape.

This was a massive risk on Rahab's part, but Rahab understood that doing the right thing sometimes means taking big risks.

Risks are part of following Jesus, even today. When you and I decide to make Christ the priority in our lives, we will have to take risks. We'll face the choices between easy roads and risky ones almost every day.

Trusting God should be something we're doing on a daily basis. Just like Rahab, we are all faced with the choice of who to believe—God or people.

Rahab chose to believe God. Now read Joshua 2:9-11 to understand what Rahab was thinking. What did Rahab believe about the Israelite God? Write her statement here:

_____

_____

Making a statement like this is no small thing. For Rahab, a prostitute, a citizen of the wicked city of Jericho, to make the choice to believe in the Israelites' God was an extraordinary step of courage and faith.

She hid the spies because she believed their God was God and that He would give them the land of Canaan. She believed it so strongly she was willing to take a huge risk, to put herself and her family in danger by concealing two strangers who had come in God's name.

In Joshua 2:12-13, what request did Rahab make and what does this tell us about her heart?

_____

_____

Don't miss how critical this moment is. Rahab is at a turning point in her life. She's just defied her king and turned her back on her city. She could have put her sole focus on herself, but she didn't. Somewhere along the way, Rahab came to understand that her life wasn't all about her. In this crisis moment, she is thinking of others.

What about you? In a crisis moment, who do you think about? Yourself or others?

Reading on in Joshua 2, the spies make a promise to Rahab in verses 17-20, giving her instructions on what to do and vowing an oath of protection. In your own words, write the instructions Rahab must follow to be protected from Jericho's coming destruction:

_____

_____

> Rahab said something very important in Joshua 2:21.
>
> **"According to your words, so be it."**
>
> Remember, Rahab wasn't an Israelite. She had never seen God do a miracle. But in her heart, she had come to the place where she believed that God was the true God.
>
> Read her words out loud. Are you brave enough to say this to God like Rahab did?

When the spies left, Rahab obeyed immediately. Don't rush past that. She tied the scarlet cord out her window the moment they were out the door. She didn't wait to make sure her neighbors weren't watching. She didn't stop to check with her landlord. Those were the instructions she had received if she and her family wanted to be saved, and she obeyed.

Right away.

Like Rahab, are you willing to stand bold and confidently say to God, "According to your words, so be it"?

_____

Are you living in delayed obedience (which is really just disobedience)?

_____

What will it take for you to stand boldly for Christ in obedience to His Word?

_____

Who Else Said It?

The phrase "According to your words, so be it" isn't unique to Rahab. The concept has been spoken out loud by many other people throughout Scripture. Let's meet some of them and find out what they said.

Scripture	Who Is Speaking?	What Did They Say?
Matthew 6:10		
Matthew 26:39		
Luke 1:38		
Luke 22:42		
Acts 21:14		
James 4:15		

If you had been in Rahab's place, what would your answer have been?

- ☐ I need to ask my friends for advice first.
- ☐ I'm afraid of making a mistake. Let me pray about it for a few days.
- ☐ I'll do it, but let me find the perfect rope to use first.
- ☐ Other: _____

Out of the entire city of Jericho, God could only find one woman who was receptive to His truth. Write one of my favorite Bible verses, 1 Chronicles 16:9, in the space provided and be encouraged!

While the rest of Jericho saw Rahab's past, God saw Rahab's heart. He chose her for this very moment in time for a specific purpose, which would have far-reaching affect. If God needed you right now for His work, how would he find your heart?

- ☐ Not available
- ☐ Half-hearted
- ☐ Fully devoted but fearful
- ☐ Fully devoted

How can you grow in your faith as you continue this study? What actions can you take today to boldly stand for Christ like Rahab?

When we have faith in God and choose to be obedient, our faith will be as visible as the scarlet cord hanging out Rahab's window.

Four chapters later, in Joshua 4, the Israelite army reaches Jericho, and God gives them the battle strategy. Of course, when God revealed His plan, everybody had to be in shock. Some folks probably even thought it was a joke, that Joshua was pulling their legs just before they marched against the most heavily fortified city in all of Canaan.

Can you hear it?

"Ha ha, Joshua! March around in circles. That's a good one! What's the real plan?"

Can you imagine their faces when Joshua told them that *was* the plan? And, what was more, they had to do it for six days? And then on the seventh day, they got to blow trumpets!

Really intimidating, right?

But hey, this generation had learned their parents' lesson. When God gives you a command, you obey it. And they did.

Picture it. The Israelite army marching around the walls of Jericho in tight formation, in silence, no music, no cheering, no sound except the pounding of their feet against the dirt. And there, in the distance, draped from a window on the outside wall, a scarlet cord danced in the wind.

The army would have known. Maybe not on the first day, but definitely by the second day. Joshua would have told them. The spies would have told them.

That scarlet cord couldn't have been hidden. It would have stood out glaringly obvious against the stone walls. Unmistakable.

Rahab had followed instructions. And now the whole nation of Israel knew about it. They knew her story. They knew how much faith she had. And they believed that God would preserve her life and her family's life because she had obeyed Him.

That's not something Rahab did for herself. Yes, she chose to obey, but her actions were an outside display of a change that had already taken place in her heart. No longer was she Rahab the Harlot. She was Rahab the Chosen One. She was Rahab, the woman who put her faith on display for the whole world to see.

Her steps of obedience did more than just move her out of Jericho. God was going to transform her life into something no one had ever seen before.

When we accept a personal relationship with Jesus Christ, God starts changing us from the inside out.

Look up 1 Corinthians 6:11 and write it here:

_____

Finish reading Joshua 6:22-25.

Jericho comes crumbling down in a big way, but there's one section of the wall still standing. And it's the section with the scarlet cord hanging from the window. Rahab and her family have been saved. What sort of influence do you think that had on everyone involved?

If you were Rahab, what would you think?

_____

If you were Rahab's family, what would you think?

_____

If you were one of the Israelite soldiers, marching around the walls for a week, and then the whole city came crashing down except for the house with the red cord, what would you think?

_____

Jericho is a powerful lesson in obedience no matter where this story finds you. Maybe you're in a place where you desperately need a wall to come crashing down. Or maybe you're in a place where you desperately need your walls to keep standing.

If you think about it, in our story, obedience and faith in God solved both problems at the same time. The Israelites' obedience and faith in God cause the walls of Jericho to crumble. Likewise, Rahab's obedience and faith in God kept her walls standing.

Once Rahab and her family were rescued from the ruins of Jericho, they joined the nation of Israel, but God still wasn't done with Rahab yet. He was still working on her, and He had an even bigger plan for her life. Rahab shows up again in the Bible, in Hebrews 11:31 and in James 2:25.

Look up Hebrews 11:31. What was it that kept Rahab from being destroyed?

_____

Look up James 2:25. What showed that Rahab was right with God?

_____

What great things has the Lord done for you and your family that can encourage others?

_____

_____

God took Rahab's past of pain, sin, and shame and cleansed her completely from the inside out with a reward at the end. It didn't matter what her life had been like before she came to Him. It didn't matter what she had done. God doesn't play favorites, and He never turns away anyone who comes to Him sincerely.

Maybe you have a secret that only you and God know about, and you can't imagine ever being forgiven for it. Whether it's stealing, sex, drugs, alcohol, gluttony, or something else, just remember that there are no impossible cases for God.

> Now would be a great time to talk to God in prayer. Hand your secrets over. Give them all to the Lord. If Rahab can be forgiven and blessed, so can you.

Remember the Before and After section yesterday? Let's do that again with Rahab.

RAHAB (Joshua 2)

Before God's Rescue – Rahab was a pagan prostitute. She worshipped the false god Ra, and she lived as an outcast among her own people.

After God's Rescue – Rahab becomes a hero of faith among the nation of Israel, and she is regarded with honor and admiration even today.

Select your favorite verse from Day 2 then flip forward to Day 5 of this chapter and record it in the top box. For the rest of today spend time in prayer meditating and living out the verse you selected.

A Prayer

Jesus, heal my brokenness. I confess I need a life change like Rahab. I can't hide my sin from You another minute. Forgive me, Lord. Change me and move me forward. I don't want to be stuck anymore. I give You complete permission to move to my heart and make me new from the inside out. Fill my life with peace through Your grace and mercy. I need You and praise You, Lord, my Savior and Redeemer. Amen!

Day 3: I Signed Up to Make a Difference

Everyone has a purpose. If you know Jesus, you know you were made for a specific reason, to accomplish a specific goal, and most believers try to discover that purpose through volunteering in their community or in their churches.

Ah! Volunteer work. It can be rewarding, uplifting, enlightening—and exhausting.

Maybe you volunteered to deliver an elder's groceries, and you ended up cleaning his house instead. Maybe you offered to give a friend a ride to the airport, and you ended up having to help them carry in their luggage too. Maybe you stepped up to open doors for people at your church, but when you got there, they needed you in the nursery more—so instead of shaking hands, you're changing diapers.

In the middle of all of it, all you think is: "I didn't sign up for this!"

Have you ever been there? I have. It can be really frustrating when you're trying to do what you believe God has called you to do, and nothing seems to be working out.

What did you do the last time you volunteered to help someone?

_____

What did you learn about yourself? About God?

_____

Nobody volunteers to help someone else because they're bored. It's possible that boredom can move people to do some crazy things, but when you choose to give up your time, to spend your energy investing in someone else's needs, it's not because you're out of things to do. It's because you want to make a difference.

Somewhere deep inside all of us there's a yearning to matter. We want our lives to mean something, to leave a legacy that's bigger than our own story.

Some of us haven't found our purpose yet. We've been searching for years, trying different things, going to counseling or talking with experts. And nothing is happening.

Others of us have found our purpose—or what we think is our purpose—but the more we invest, the less successful it is or the more stressed-out and exhausted we become. It's not what we thought it would be. It's not working at all.

Where are you in the process of discovering your purpose? Highlight the statement that most closely matches where you are today.

I don't think I have a purpose.	I have a purpose, but I can't find it.	I know my purpose, but I don't know the next step.	I'm living my purpose, but I'm ready to give up.

Let me encourage you. You were created for a reason. You matter to God, enough that He knows the number of hairs on your head. There's nothing you have gone through in your life that God doesn't know about, and He deeply desires to be part of your life.

You have a purpose, and you can make a difference.

One person, walking side-by-side with Jesus, can turn the world upside down. Who knows? Maybe that's your purpose.

Salt and Light

Jesus put it this way in Matthew 5:13-15 (NLT).

> "You are the salt of the earth. But what good is salt if it
> has lost its flavor? Can you make it useful again? It will be
> thrown out and trampled underfoot as worthless. You are

the light of the world—like a city on a hilltop that cannot be hidden. No one lights a lamp and then puts it under a basket. Instead, a lamp is placed on a stand, where it gives light to everyone in the house."

Salt is everywhere. In everything. It's in you, and it's in me. Some of us have more than our healthy share of it, frankly. You've heard the phrase "worth his salt"?

Historically, salt is one of the most important minerals in the world. People used salt to preserve meats. Doctors used it to sterilize wounds (ouch!). To this day, salt is valuable for the enhancement of flavors in food that it provides.

And we couldn't live without. The human body needs salt. Common, ordinary, ubiquitous salt is potentially the most important element in history.

Jesus compared His people to salt for a number of reasons, mostly because salt has a purpose that never goes away. And so do Jesus-followers. Maybe there are millions of us, billions of us, but each one of us has been specifically created to do God's work, to be Jesus to other people, to stand up and be salt and light in a world that doesn't know the truth.

If you've got salt, be salty!

If you've got light, shine!

Do you know a salty Christian? Meaning, do you know someone who has totally embraced the idea of being Jesus to others? Write down what you've noticed about that person.

What makes them like the salt Jesus is talking about?

_____

_____

_____

Jesus also calls His children the Light of the World. We know Him, and He is the true Light, the source of truth. Our job is to share that light with the rest of the world.

But that's not easy. Talking about Jesus with people who don't know Him is scary, and it's so much easier to hide our little candle flame under a basket so we won't draw too much attention.

Friend, that's not why we're here.

You may have a greater purpose beyond just being a light for Jesus, but every Christ-follower has this in common. We are all lights in the darkness, and none of us should be hiding.

Spend time praying. Talk to Jesus. Tell Him your worries and your fears. Turn on your music app and sing worship songs to God at the top of your lungs. Step out in faith and do something for another person who can't pay you back.

List a few things you can do today that will help your flame burn brighter.

_____

_____

You can make a difference as a follower of Jesus. He has given us His power, and He is walking right beside us, ready, willing, and able to help us through life's challenges as our Friend as well as our Savior.

"If you will find your purpose, you will find your passion." - Steven Furtick

Knowing Your Purpose

Let's say you're one of the fortunate few who have discovered your life's purpose. You know exactly where you are. You know exactly what God has promised you, and you are rip-roaring-ready to go change the world.

Awesome! As Jesus-followers, we have that opportunity.

If you're walking in your purpose right now and you have passion in your purpose, don't allow others to drag you down. Surround yourself with people who admire your passion or who are passionate as well. Build a community of friends who are on the same page, who speak the same language, and who are all on fire for what you care about.

Just remember one thing. Following Jesus can be a risky business, and it requires that we trust Him completely.

It means we trust Him when the road He has us walking is rocky and difficult.

It means we trust Him when we have to wait longer than we anticipated.

It means we trust Him when our purpose doesn't come together in the way we planned.

It means that in the moments when we don't feel like it, we're willing to share our God story with the people in our lives.

Passion IN Our Purpose

Many times, those of us who discover our purpose and start living it run into another problem that we didn't foresee—Our passion for our purpose evaporates.

Maybe you love hiking. You love everything about it. You live and breathe hiking, and God's purpose for your life is hiking—or some variation thereof.

If all you do is hike, you're going to get tired of it. Your purpose in life may be to hike the mountain trails, but if you aren't passionate about it anymore, you're going to want to give up.

This is why it's important to have passion *in* your purpose. Maybe you love hiking, but if *all* you love is hiking, it'll get old after a while. Instead, maybe your passion should be helping others encounter God through a nature hike or running for fundraisers that benefit the poor or sick. Passion in your purpose will carry you much farther than just purpose alone.

Most of us start with our passion. Our passion usually comes before our purpose, but somewhere along the road we get so caught up in our purpose that we leave our passion behind.

That's important to note. We never lose our passion. We leave it. We forget it.

Read Revelation 2:2-5 (ESV) below.

> "I know your works, your toil and your patient endurance, and how you cannot bear with those who are evil, but have tested those who call themselves apostles and are not, and found them to be false. I know you are enduring patiently and bearing up for my name's sake, and you have not grown weary. But I have this against you, that you have abandoned the love you had at first. Remember therefore from where you have fallen; repent, and do the works you

did at first. If not, I will come to you and remove your lampstand from its place, unless you repent."

Look at verse 4 again: *You have abandoned the love you had at first.*

That's what happens when you leave your passion behind as you pursue your purpose. When you walk off and forget your passion, you'll run the risk of burning out.

So what if you've forgotten your passion? How do you find again? Easy. You practice it.

Is your passion your friends? Then practice being friendly.

Do you need love for your spouse? Practice showing love toward your spouse.

Do you need encouragement? Practice being an encourager to others.

You can find your passion again. Just begin at the beginning. Look back to where you started. How did you discover your purpose? Remember, your passion usually predates your purpose.

What are you passionate about?

_____

How can you integrate your passion with your purpose?

_____

Select your favorite verse from Day 3 then flip forward to Day 5 of this chapter and record it in the top box. For the rest of today spend time in prayer meditating and living out the verse you selected.

A Prayer

Dear Heavenly Father, open my eyes to the divine opportunities You alone provide for me. I want to make a difference and use my talents for Your glory, but I don't know how to get started. Show me. Guide me. Put me on the right path to You. I'm yours, God. I want Your name to be Glorified in my life. Not my will but Yours be done in my life. Amen!

Day 4: You Are Loved

Love has a way of changing people. It's one of those peculiar parts about human life that keeps it so interesting.

Do you know what it's like to be loved? Not just by your family but by someone who isn't obligated to love you? Someone who chooses to love you?

It's a different kind of love than what you experience with your parents or your children. Love like that has the power to change the way you see yourself, the people around you, and your potential. Knowing that someone loves you and truly believing it gives a person confidence, security, and boldness like they didn't have before. ***God loves you.***

Do you really get that? Do any of us? He isn't obligated to do anything. He isn't under anyone else's authority. God does what He wants, and no one can stop Him. No one has the right to stop Him. And He chooses to love us in spite of ourselves.

More than that, God wants you to love Him back. He wants a love relationship with You. He's done the impossible, the extraordinary, the unbelievable to make a way for us to communicate with Him face to face, one on one, no barriers, no walls, no fear.

---

10 Facts about Jesus' Love for You

1. You were created in God's likeness, and His plans are designed with your best interests in mind.
2. Because you are loved unconditionally by the One who made the universe, you can trust your future in God's hands.
3. God loves you and desires to have a personal relationship with you. That means daily connections about everything that matters to you, because it matters to Him too.
4. God desires for each human being to love Him and acknowledge Him as the source of their joy and salvation.

> 5. God sees you as extremely valuable and worthwhile. Do you know how much He values you? So much that He sent Jesus to the Earth from heaven to die for our sins so we can spend eternity with him.
> 6. You matter to God.
> 7. God has given us more grace than we can ever comprehend.
> 8. Look up 1 Corinthians 2:9 and write it somewhere you will see it every day.
> 9. If Jesus had a refrigerator, your picture would be hanging on it for everyone to admire. He is so proud of you!
> 10. **You are treasured by the Lord!**

Which one of those ten facts means the most to you? Why?

_____

Recognizing the facts above and believing they are truth helps us tell ourselves the truth and not lies. We shouldn't talk to ourselves as though we are worthless, without value, unimportant, or insignificant. None of those things are true. So when negative thoughts like that begin to whisper through your mind, remember these ten facts.

Talking negatively about yourself and to yourself doesn't please God. You're His child. He loves you. You are unique, special, important, and valuable to Him.

It's time to start seeing yourself that way.

> **"No one who has ever lived or is living now or will ever live can accomplish your unique purpose. This is something only you can do . . . something only God can do through you." – June Hunt**

Accepting God's unconditional love may be the hardest thing you've ever done, but if you want to discover your true purpose, God's love is the key.

You can only know and understand your purpose as you listen and hear from the Holy Spirit—God who lives inside you. And you can only hear from God through the Holy Spirit through an intimate love relationship with Him.

> What often happens when God begins to work around us is that we become self-centered. We begin trying to manage what is happening or to expand upon and administer it. We must reorient our lives to God, to see life from His perspective. We must allow Him to develop His character in us and let Him reveal His thoughts to us. Only then can we gain a proper perspective on life. When you're God-centered, even the desires to do things that please God come from God's stirring in your heart. The Bible says, "It is God who is working in you, enabling you both to will and to act for His good purpose." Philippians 2:13

The "Silent" Partner

When we go to church, we usually hear about God the Father. And most of us will hear about Jesus, the Son. But how many of us really get an opportunity to learn about the third member of the Trinity—the Holy Spirit? Sometimes He's called the Holy Ghost. But if you compare how much the church talks about Him to how much we talk about the other two members of the Trinity, we might as well call the Holy Spirit the Silent Partner.

In all honesty, sometimes the Holy Spirit is a little too much for Christians. He makes us nervous. We have all ignored the Holy Spirit for way too long. We have either ignored Him because we are afraid to be overpowered by a charismatic feeling, or we avoid Him altogether because we don't understand Him.

Well, let's deal with that right now. What does the Holy Spirit actually do?

1. He knows the future (John 16:13)
2. He places each member in the church for service (1 Corinthians 12:18)
3. He reminds us of what Jesus has already revealed and helps apply the truth to your lives today. (John 14:26)

4. He brings you comfort (John 14:16)
5. He brings you understanding (1 Corinthians 2:14)
6. He reveals truth (John 16:13)

Which of the jobs of the Holy Spirit means the most to you? Why?

_____

> Stop what you're doing and speak to the Holy Spirit. Ask Him to be as much a part of your life as Jesus is.

Once we know and recognize the Holy Spirit in our lives, we can start listening to God's voice in a much more effective way. The Holy Spirit *is* God. So why aren't we listening to Him?

Here are four steps that will help you hear God's voice and discover His will, His plan, and His purpose for your life:

1. Resist and rebuke the negative talk in your head with God's truth.

God's truth is like a sword. It cuts through every lie and slices away the layers of confusion that keep us in a haze.

Review the ten facts about Jesus' love for you. Now, in the space below, write the fact that you will use the next time the enemy starts whispering lies in your ear.

_____

_____

2. Memorize Scripture about spiritual warfare and finding God's truth.

We are in a battle right now. Did you know that? Part of following Jesus is standing up against our enemy, who wants to destroy us. We are in a constant battle for our focus, our perspective, our mindset, and our joy. Satan would love nothing more than to distract us from what

Jesus has planned for our lives, and the best weapon to use against him is the Bible.

Study the Bible and find verses that speak to you. Need a verse to start with? Try Romans 8:37. Write it in the lines provided and start memorizing it today.

_____

_____

_____

3. Learn to recognize the Holy Spirit's leading and voice.

The more time you spend reading the Bible, the easier it will be for you to identify the Holy Spirit when He is speaking. The same is true when you spend time in prayer and in worship, whether through music or service projects.

Spend time with God. Don't just read stories about the heroes of Scripture. Learn from them. Apply the truth that the Holy Spirit reveals. Before you know it, it won't be difficult to hear God's voice.

4. Connect with the Holy Spirit's presence.

The Holy Spirit is a person, just like God, just like Jesus. The first step you can take to connecting with Him is to stop referring to Him as *It*. Acknowledge the Holy Spirit as God Himself. Then, invite Him into your day. Welcome Him into your life.

He's already there. But the more you acknowledge His presence in your life, the more aware of Him you'll be. And the easier you'll find it to connect with Him.

So now what?

What will you do with this information? Maybe you've never heard this about the Holy Spirit before. Maybe you already knew it, but you'd never taken time to truly let it sink in.

It is my deepest desire that you will grow closer to the Holy Spirit and long to know Jesus more in your heart. The closer you desire to be to Jesus, the more time you intentionally spend with Him, the more often you will hear the Holy Spirit and experience His presence in your life. And when you experience His presence, you'll be able to take the next step toward discovering God's true purpose for your life.

> *"The first step towards getting somewhere is to decide you're not going to stay where you are."*
> *- John Pierpont "J.P." Morgan.*

Select your favorite verse from Day 4 then flip forward to Day 5 of this chapter and record it in the top box. For the rest of today spend time in prayer meditating and living out the verse you selected.

A Prayer

Holy Spirit, forgive me for not including You in my prayer life. It's strange, but I didn't realize I was ignoring You. But today is a new day. Help me. Remind me. Transform me. I give my "what ifs" and "if onlys" to You today. Forgive my confusion about my purpose. I am constantly fighting my negative thoughts and doubts. Keep me close to Your heart and help me believe the promises of God are true. When the enemy tells me I'm alone and unloved, shout loudly into my heart the truth of Scripture. God loves me, and I am not alone. Thank You for living inside of my soul and giving me the comfort I need. Amen!

Day 5: Hand in Hand WITH God

As you complete each daily section of this study, write down your favorite verse from each day.

Day 1: _____

Day 2: _____

Day 3: _____

Day 4: _____

Journal the Journey:

1. What aspects of your relationship with God and finding your purpose have become a little clearer?
2. As you are listening to God's voice, what is He asking you to do? Is it something huge or something small? Remember, little things matter to God. He may ask you to do something small first.
3. Where do you see God working in your life right now?

A Prayer

Thank You, Lord, for revealing how much You love me and will provide for me. I can have peace about my future because You have the future in Your hands, and the best is yet to come. Help me live a refreshed and hopeful life where I am right now. I want to always walk in the assurance of Your love for me. You have done so much for me, and I want to live my life for You. All that needed to be done for my salvation was done on the cross. Use me to lead others to You. Use my hands, feet, or mouth to make a difference in this world. For Your Glory! In Your precious name I pray, amen!

Mentoring Tip: God is always pursuing you. You can trust that He has a plan and a purpose for your life.

APPENDIX A: MENTOR/LEADER GUIDE

Please read the introduction before you begin this Mentor/Leader guide.

The following information will help you be equipped to mentor or leader others through this 8-Week Session Bible Study.

UNDERSTAND YOUR ROLE AS MENTOR/LEADER

God does not require anyone to have a Seminary Degree or years experience mentoring or leading others. Your role is to be:

- A Christ follower, who is further down the road in your walk with the Lord and still growing spiritually
- Be a good listener and willing to share your God stories
- Available to come alongside the next generation to guide and encourage
- Following God's agenda and not your own.

Through this Bible Study, Jayme will provide inspiring stories, specific ways to dig deeper into God's Word and discussion questions for conversations to apply to your life. As a Mentor or Leader you are presenting the truths in God's Word and intentionally being present in others lives. You are relying on God to move and stretch the other person(s) into becoming the person God created them to be. For each session and conversation you are simply being Jesus with skin on.

UNDERSTAND YOUR ROLE AS A MENTEE/
SMALL GROUP MEMBER

If you are one of the following you are a mentee/member:

- Eager to know God in a deeper way and grow spiritually
- Approachable on any topic or situation
- Willing to be vulnerable and step out of your comfort zone
- Desiring to learn more about God's Word and applying it to your life on a daily basis.

When you make the choice to become a part of a mentoring relationship or small group you will gain confidence in your faith, insight into Scripture, discernment for decision-making and Forward motion with your Savior.

PRAYER

An essential part of this Bible Study is prayer. This Study is a spiritual journey with Jesus Christ and the Holy Spirit, who will lead you as you pray. I encourage you to invite Him into the meeting each week. Pray for wisdom and discernment. Pray for the Holy Spirit to speak in and through you. *Side By Side* was created to help you as you help others to grow in their faith in Christ. Plan to open and close each session with prayer and include the Holy Spirit to be in control of all conversations.

SCHEDULE A TIME AND PLACE

A mentoring relationship or small group can happen any time of the day or night that is convenient for the people involved. Meeting on a consistent basis is key to success in each relationship/group. I recommend 60 minutes or less for all Mentoring relationship sessions and 90 minutes for all small group sessions.

Mentoring relationships may meet in a coffee cafe, casual restaurant or café (preferably one that you walk up to the counter, order and pick up as you are seated), lobby of church or work, or walking in a park.

PREPARING FOR EACH NEW SESSION

- Study and complete your weekly Conversation Chapter before the session begins.
- Spend time everyday praying for the Mentor/Leader/Mentees in your life.
- Respect each other's time. Arrive and end on time for each session.
- Come to each session dedicated to learning and anticipating the Lord to move.
- Review Day 5 for the particular Conversation Chapter you will be discussing for the session and reread your selected Bible verses.
- Invite the Holy Spirit to lead your session and give Him complete permission to move in you in a mighty way.
- Be willing to approach each conversation honestly and thoughtfully.
- Close each session with one Call To Action assignment and prayer.

APPENDIX B: SCRIPTURE INDEX

Reference	Ch.	Day	Chart	Reference	Ch.	Day	Chart
1 Chronicles 16:34	6	1	God's Promises Chart	John 12:1-2	5	4	Jesus' Life Examples
1 Chronicles 16:8-11, 23-24	3	3	Circle One	John 12:47	2	4	Condemn vs Convict Chart
1 Corinthians 1:2	6	1	God's Promises Chart	John 14:16	7	4	
1 Corinthians 1:9	6	3	Who God Is Chart	John 14:16	8	4	Holy Spirit's Job
1 Corinthians 12:18	8	4	Holy Spirit's Job	John 14:26	8	4	Holy Spirit's Job
1 Corinthians 13	3	4		John 15:14-15	4	3	God's Promise Chart
1 Corinthians 2:14	8	4	Holy Spirit's Job	John 15:15	4	4	Verse Match Rainbow
1 Corinthians 2:9	8	4	10 Facts About Jesus' Love	John 15:4-5	2	2	
1 Corinthians 3:8	3	4		John 15:7	1	1	
1 Corinthians 6:11	8	2		John 16:13	8	4	Holy Spirit's Job
1 Corinthians 6:19-20	5	3	Fence Chart	John 16:13	8	4	Holy Spirit's Job
1 Corinthians 6:20	7	5	Memorization	John 21:20-22	3	1	Key Verse
1 John 1:2	6	1	God's Promises Chart	John 4:24	6	3	Who God Is Chart
1 John 1:5	6	3	Who God Is Chart	John 6:35	1	2	Names of God Chart
1 John 1:9	2	4	Condemn vs Convict Chart	John 15:16	3	4	You and God Chart
1 John 2:1	1	2	Names of God Chart	Jonah 2:2	6	1	God's Promises Chart

1 John 3:1	3	4		Joshua 2	8	2	Rahab's Story
1 John 4:16	6	3	Who God Is Chart	Joshua 2	8	2	Rahab Before & After
1 John 4:9-10	7	5	Memorization	Joshua 2:12-13	8	2	
1 Kings 17:12	1	3		Joshua 2:17-20	8	2	
1 Kings 17:14	1	3		Joshua 2:1-8	8	2	
1 Kings 17:15-16	1	3		Joshua 2:21	8	2	Just Say It
1 Kings 17:8-16	1	3		Joshua 2:9-11	8	2	
1 Kings 17:9-10	1	3		Joshua 23:14	6	1	God's Promises Chart
1 Kings 8:23	6	1	God's Promises Chart	Joshua 4	8	2	
1 Peter 2:20	7	2		Joshua 6:22-25	8	2	
1 Peter 3:15-16	1	4		Jude 1:24	6	1	God's Promises Chart
1 Peter 3:8-9	3	4		Judges 2:10	5	1	
1 Peter 5:7	2	4	Condemn vs Convict Chart	Judges 2:18-19	5	1	Cycle Chart
1 Peter 5:7	6	1	God's Promises Chart	Judges 3:31	5	1	
1 Samuel 14:1-15	6	2		Judges 6:12	6	1	God's Promises Chart
1 Samuel 14:12	6	2		Judges 6:24	1	2	Names of God Chart
1 Samuel 14:12-13	6	2		Lamentations 3:25	6	1	Hope Is Chart
1 Samuel 14:4	6	2		Lamentations 3:32	6	1	God's Promises Chart
1 Samuel 14:5-6	6	2		Leviticus 26:11	6	1	God's Promises Chart
1 Samuel 15 - 2 Samuel	8	1	David Before & After	Luke 1:38	8	2	Who Else Said It?
1 Samuel 16:7	2	1		Luke 10:20	6	4	Lamb's Book of Life
1 Samuel 16:7	3	4	You and God Chart	Luke 12:6-7	1	2	
1 Samuel 17:17-22	2	1		Luke 18:16	3	3	

1 Samuel 17:22	2	1	Key Verse	Luke 18:1-8	6	1	God's Promises Chart
1 Samuel 2:30	6	1	God's Promises Chart	Luke 22:42	8	2	Who Else Said It?
1 Samuel 30:6	6	4	B-Attitudes	Luke 24:13-35	1	2	
1 Thessalonians 1:3	6	1	Hope Is Chart	Luke 6:12-16	5	4	Jesus' Life Examples
1 Thessalonians 4:16	6	1	God's Promises Chart	Malachi 3:16	1	1	
1 Thessalonians 5:11	1	1		Malachi 3:16-17	1	1	Key Verse
1 Thessalonians 5:18	6	4	B-Attitudes	Malachi 3:16-17	4	2	
1 Thessalonians 5:8	6	1	Hope Is Chart	Malachi 3:17	1	2	
1 Timothy 1:1	6	4		Malachi 3:6-7	6	1	God's Promises Chart
1 Timothy 1:15	6	1	God's Promises Chart	Mark 1:35-38	5	4	Jesus' Life Examples
1 Timothy 2:1-5	2	2		Mark 14:35-36	5	4	Jesus' Life Examples
1 Timothy 4:16	5	3	Fence Chart	Mark 14:3-9	4	2	
1 Timothy 6:4	3	3	Envy and Strife	Mark 2:1-12	6	1	God's Promises Chart
1 Timothy 6:6	3	4		Mark 6:31	4	4	4 helpful tips chart
2 Chronicles 16:9	6	1	God's Promises Chart	Mark 6:31	5	1	Key Verse
2 Corinthians 1:21	8	1		Matthew 1:5	8	2	
2 Corinthians 1:8-9	7	2		Matthew 1:5-6, 16	8	2	Ruth's Family Tree
2 Corinthians 10:4	2	4	Condemn vs Convict Chart	Matthew 11:28	6	1	God's Promises Chart
2 Corinthians 11:24-27	6	1		Matthew 11:28-30	5	2	
2 Corinthians 11:30	6	1		Matthew 18:19-20	1	2	
2 Corinthians 12:8-9	2	2		Matthew 22:32	6	3	Who God Is Chart
2 Corinthians 2:14	4	2		Matthew 22:37-39	7	5	Memorization

209

2 Corinthians 3:16-18	2	4		Matthew 26:36-38	5	4	Jesus' Life Examples
2 Corinthians 5:15	7	5	Memorization	Matthew 26:39	8	2	Who Else Said It?
2 Corinthians 5:17	5	3	Fence Chart	Matthew 28:20	3	4	You and God Chart
2 Corinthians 5:17	6	1	God's Promises Chart	Matthew 5:13-15	8	3	
2 John 1:2	6	1	God's Promises Chart	Matthew 5:37	5	3	
2 Kings 5:15	6	1	God's Promises Chart	Matthew 5:37	5	4	
2 Peter 1:4	6	1	God's Promises Chart	Matthew 5:9	3	3	
2 Samuel 22:31	6	1	God's Promises Chart	Matthew 6:10	8	2	Who Else Said It?
2 Thessalonians 1:5-10	6	1	God's Promises Chart	Matthew 6:33	5	3	Fence Chart
2 Timothy 1:7	6	1	God's Promises Chart	Matthew 6:6	3	4	You and God Chart
2 Timothy 4:7	4	1		Matthew 7:7	4	4	4 helpful tips chart
3 John 1:11	6	1	God's Promises Chart	Matthew 9:22	3	2	I Think vs God Says Chart
Acts 10:34	6	3	Who God Is Chart	Micah 6:8	6	1	God's Promises Chart
Acts 16:13-15	5	3		Micah 7:18-19	2	4	Condemn vs Convict Chart
Acts 16:31	7	2		Micah 7:19	2	3	
Acts 17:27-28	6	1	God's Promises Chart	Nahum 1:7	6	1	God's Promises Chart
Acts 21:14	8	2	Who Else Said It?	Nehemiah 8:10	6	1	God's Promises Chart
Amos 3:7	4	4	Verse Match Rainbow	Numbers 14:18	6	1	God's Promises Chart
Amos 3:7	6	1	God's Promises Chart	Numbers 23:19	6	3	Who God Is Chart
Amos 5:14	8	1		Obadiah 1:15	6	1	God's Promises Chart

Reference			Chart	Reference			Chart
Colossians 1:23	6	1	Hope Is Chart	Philemon 1:25	6	1	God's Promises Chart
Colossians 1:27	6	1	God's Promises Chart	Philippians 1:6	3	4	You and God Chart
Colossians 2:13-14	2	5		Philippians 1:6	6	1	God's Promises Chart
Colossians 3:1-4	3	4		Philippians 3:13-15	4	1	Key Verse
Colossians 3:2	3	1		Philippians 3:14	4	1	
Daniel 12:1	6	4	Lamb's Book of Life	Philippians 4:11-13	3	4	
Daniel 9:4	6	1	God's Promises Chart	Philippians 4:13	2	3	
Deuteronomy 2:7	8	1	Key Verse	Philippians 4:19	3	4	You and God Chart
Deuteronomy 2:7	8	1		Philippians 4:3	6	4	Lamb's Book of Life
Deuteronomy 3:22	6	1	God's Promises Chart	Philippians 4:6	1	3	
Deuteronomy 31:6	7	3		Philippians 4:6-7	5	2	
Deuteronomy 4:31	6	3	Who God Is Chart	Philippians 4:8	2	4	
Deuteronomy 5:1-5	8	1		Proverbs 1:33	5	3	
Ecclesiastes 3:11	6	1	God's Promises Chart	Proverbs 10:19	7	4	Words Have Power
Ephesians 1:4	5	1		Proverbs 11:12	7	4	Words Have Power
Ephesians 2:10	3	2	I Think vs God Says Chart	Proverbs 13:3	7	4	Words Have Power
Ephesians 2:10	3	5	Journaling the Journey	Proverbs 14:30	3	1	
Ephesians 2:4,6	2	4	Condemn vs Convict Chart	Proverbs 15:1	7	4	Words Have Power
Ephesians 3:20	6	1	God's Promises Chart	Proverbs 15:29	1	1	
Ephesians 6:10	5	1	Prayer	Proverbs 15:3	7	1	3 Big O Descriptions
Esther 2:23	1	1		Proverbs 16:24	7	4	Words Have Power
Esther 4:13-14	1	4		Proverbs 16:25	5	2	

Esther 4:14	6	1	God's Promises Chart	Proverbs 16:3	6	1	God's Promises Chart
Esther 6:1	1	1		Proverbs 16:9	4	2	
Exodus 1	2	2	Deeper Look	Proverbs 18:13	7	4	Words Have Power
Exodus 15:26	1	2	Names of God Chart	Proverbs 19:14	7	4	Words Have Power
Exodus 2:10	2	2		Proverbs 21:23	7	4	Words Have Power
Exodus 2:1-10	2	2		Proverbs 29:11	7	4	Words Have Power
Exodus 2:5-9	2	2		Proverbs 29:20	7	4	Words Have Power
Exodus 3 - Deuteronomy 24	8	1	Moses Before & After	Proverbs 3:5-6	6	4	B-Attitudes
Exodus 33:14	6	1	God's Promises Chart	Proverbs 3:5-6	7	4	
Exodus 34:6	6	3	Who God Is Chart	Proverbs 31	7	2	Story of Emilie Barnes
Ezekiel 36:26	6	1	God's Promises Chart	Proverbs 4:23	5	3	Fence Chart
Ezekiel 48:35	1	2	Names of God Chart	Psalm 107:20	7	3	
Ezra 8:22	6	1	God's Promises Chart	Psalm 109:26	7	4	
Galatians 1:3-4	6	1	God's Promises Chart	Psalm 118:6	5	1	
Galatians 5:6	7	5	Memorization	Psalm 121:1-2	4	4	Verse Match Rainbow
Genesis 1:1-23	5	2		Psalm 126:5-6	7	3	
Genesis 16:13	1	2	Names of God Chart	Psalm 127:2	5	2	
Genesis 18:14	6	1	God's Promises Chart	Psalm 139	3	2	I Think vs God Says Chart
Genesis 22:14	1	2	Names of God Chart	Psalm 139:13-14	3	3	
Genesis 26:24	8	1		Psalm 139:1-6	7	1	Key Verse
Genesis 29:15-35	3	2		Psalm 139:1-6	7	1	Inductive Training
Genesis 29:16-17	3	2		Psalm 139:5	7	1	
Genesis 29:20-25	3	2		Psalm 146:5	6	1	Just Say It
Genesis 30 - 50	8	1	Joseph Before & After	Psalm 23	5	1	

Genesis 37	7	2	Deeper Look	Psalm 25:21	6	1	Hope Is Chart
Genesis 50:20	7	2		Psalm 25:9	4	3	God's Promise Chart
Genesis 50:20	8	2		Psalm 3:2-6	6	3	
Genesis 6:18	8	1		Psalm 31:24	6	1	Hope Is Chart
Genesis 9:12	8	1		Psalm 32:2,5	2	4	Condemn vs Convict Chart
Habakkuk 1:13	6	1	God's Promises Chart	Psalm 33:18	1	1	
Haggai 2:6	6	1	God's Promises Chart	Psalm 34:15	1	1	
Hebrews 10:22-25	1	1	Let Us Statements	Psalm 37:23	4	2	
Hebrews 10:23	6	1		Psalm 40:2	7	2	
Hebrews 10:24	1	1		Psalm 45:11	3	2	I Think vs God Says Chart
Hebrews 11:12	7	5	Memorization	Psalm 5:11	4	4	Verse Match Rainbow
Hebrews 11:31	8	2		Psalm 55:22	6	1	God's Promises Chart
Hebrews 12:1	2	1		Psalm 56	7	3	
Hebrews 4:12	6	1	God's Promises Chart	Psalm 56:3	7	3	Just Say It
Hebrews 4:16	3	4		Psalm 56:8	7	3	
Hebrews 4:16	5	3	Write Out	Psalm 71:15-24	3	3	Circle One
Hebrews 4:16	5	3	Keyword Study	Psalm 73:24	3	2	I Think vs God Says Chart
Hebrews 4:9-11	5	2		Psalm 80:7	7	3	
Hebrews 6:19	6	1	Anchor Chart	Psalm 86	7	5	Memorization
Hebrews 13:21	3	4	You and God Chart	Psalm 88	7	5	Memorization
Hosea 6:6	6	1	God's Promises Chart	Psalm 9:10	1	2	
Isaiah 26:3	6	1	God's Promises Chart	Psalm 90:12	5	3	Fence Chart
Isaiah 30:18	2	4	Condemn vs Convict Chart	Psalm 94:22	6	3	Who God Is Chart
Isaiah 30:21	5	3		Psalm 96:2-4	1	4	
Isaiah 43:25	2	2		Revelation 1:3	6	1	God's Promises Chart

213

Isaiah 46:9-10	7	1	3 Big O Descriptions	Revelation 19:11	1	2	Names of God Chart
Isaiah 48:17	2	3		Revelation 2:2-5	8	3	
Isaiah 48:17	5	3		Revelation 2:4	8	3	
Isaiah 49:15-16	1	2		Revelation 21:27	6	4	Lamb's Book of Life
Isaiah 55:11	1	5		Revelation 21:4	7	3	
Isaiah 55:8-9	7	4		Revelation 3:16	4	3	
Isaiah 63:7	3	3	Circle One	Romans 1:29	3	3	Envy and Strife
Isaiah 64:8	3	5	Journaling the Journey	Romans 11:29	2	2	
James 1:17	6	1	God's Promises Chart	Romans 11:33-36	6	2	
James 1:2-4	7	5	Memorization	Romans 11:33-36	6	3	Keyword Study
James 1:5	1	1		Romans 12:12	6	1	
James 1:5	5	1		Romans 12:2	6	1	God's Promises Chart
James 2:25	8	2		Romans 12:6-8	2	2	
James 4:15	8	2	Who Else Said It?	Romans 13:13	3	3	Envy and Strife
James 4:6	4	3	God's Promise Chart	Romans 15:13	6	1	Key Verse
James 4:7-8	4	4	Verse Match Rainbow	Romans 5:3	7	5	Memorization
Jeremiah 1:5	6	1	God's Promises Chart	Romans 5:5	6	3	Who God Is Chart
Jeremiah 14:22	6	1	Hope Is Chart	Romans 5:6-8	7	5	Memorization
Jeremiah 17:7-8	1	3		Romans 8:1	2	4	Condemn vs Convict Chart
Jeremiah 31:34	2	3		Romans 8:24b	6	4	
Jeremiah 32:27	7	1	3 Big O Descriptions	Romans 8:28	4	2	
Jeremiah 6:14	7	2		Romans 8:28	6	1	Difficult Situation Chart
Jeremiah 8:18	7	1		Romans 8:28	6	1	
Job 10:10b	5	3	Fence Chart	Romans 8:31	2	3	
Job 13:15	6	1	Hope Is Chart	Romans 8:37	8	4	
Job 19:25	6	1	God's Promises Chart	Romans 8:38	7	4	

Job 31:4	4	2		Romans 8:5-6	5	3	Fence Chart
Job 42:2	8	2		Ruth 4:14	6	1	God's Promises Chart
Joel 1:3	1	4		Ruth 4:21-22	8	2	Ruth's Family Tree
Joel 2:25	6	1	God's Promises Chart	Song of Songs 2:4	6	1	God's Promises Chart
John 1:12	6	1	God's Promises Chart	Titus 1:2	6	1	Hope Is Chart
John 1:14-18	3	4		Titus 2:11-14	3	4	
John 1:15	2	2		Titus 2:14	6	1	God's Promises Chart
John 1:17	4	5	12-Step Prayer Plan	Zechariah 2:8	6	1	God's Promises Chart
John 10:7-10	5	3		Zephaniah 3:17	6	1	God's Promises Chart
John 11:1-6	5	4	Jesus' Life Examples				
John 11:35	7	3					

APPENDIX C: MENTORING TIPS

1. **By connecting with a mentor you can do the hard work now to discover who you are and what you want.** Isaiah 58:11 (Voice)
2. **Concentrate on helping one person. Become an activated believer.** Hebrews 6:10 (NIV)
3. **God has positioned you here for a specific plan and purpose and given you unique talents and gifts to share with others.** Jeremiah 29:11 (NIV)
4. **Whatever season you're in and no matter what your schedule looks like you can tailor mentoring into your lifestyle.** Ecclesiastes 3:1(NIV)
5. **Mentoring relationships need two things: good listeners and honest conversations.** James 1:19 (NIV) and Proverbs 24:26 (NIV)
6. **The blessing comes when you cross the finish line with someone else.** Ecclesiastes 4:9-10 (NIV)
7. **When you meet face-to-face, focus on your conversation and turn off your cell phone.** Proverbs 4:25 (NIV)
8. **Be encouraged! Don't measure the size of the mountain you are facing. Instead, look to the One who can move it!** Isaiah 54:10 (NIV)
9. **Listen twice as much as you speak.** Proverbs 10:19
10. **Sharing your God stories can help inspire others.** Matthew 5:16
11. **The secret to conquering stress is a grateful heart.** Psalm 9:1 (NIV)
12. **Sometimes just taking the small steps in the right direction can be the biggest step of your life. Tiptoe if you must but take the first step.** Acts 22:10 (NASB)
13. **Whenever possible keep life simple.** Proverbs 13:10 (MSG)

14. **Uncovering the root of where and why you are stuck is part of the journey.** 2 Corinthians 10:5 (NIV)

15. **Mentors help you identify your strengths and weaknesses to step out of your comfort zone.** Isaiah 40:29 (NIV)

16. **Success can only happen when you are teachable.** Proverbs 12:1(ESV)

17. **Read the signs, be brave and ask for advice.** Jeremiah 31:21 (NIV)

18. **Men and women look at faces; but God looks at the heart.** 1 Samuel 16:7 (NIV)

19. **No matter what you are facing, don't give up!** Galatians 6:9 (NIV)

20. **Take charge of your attitude.** Philippians 2:14 (ESV)

21. **In the middle of your crazy, God's love is still amazing.** Proverbs 8:17(NIV)

22. **Just a few encouraging words can plant a seed of hope.** 1 Thessalonians 5:11(ESV)

23. **You are not invisible to God.** 2 Chronicles 16:9a (NIV)

24. **Ask yourself: what am I doing for others?** Hebrews 13:16 (NIV)

25. **Keep saying these three words: There is hope!** Psalm 147:11 (NIV)

26. **Mentoring can keep you motivated at work, home and in your spiritual life.** Hebrews 10:24-25 (NIV)

27. **Mentoring relationships need to be a safe place to ask questions and share your doubts.** Mark 9:24 (NIV)

28. **A Mentor can help you see God at work, even in the difficulties.** Philippians 2:13 (NIV)

29. **Be encouraged! God can use you right where you are.** 1 Corinthians 1:26-27 (NIV)

30. **Transformation happens when you invest in other people.** Galatians 6:10 (NIV)

31. **A Mentor leads the way to a smoother path with God's Word as your guide.** Proverbs 3:5-6 (NIV)

32. **A mentor sees your potential and encourages you in the right direction.** Psalm 119:133 (NIV)

33. **A mentor isn't afraid to talk about the tough issues or ask the hard questions.** Matthew 7:7 (NIV)

34. **A mentor can't tell you what your calling is, but they can walk with you in discovering it.** 1 Thessalonians 5:24 (NIV)

35. **Mentors keep you accountable.** Proverbs 27:17 (NIV)

36. **Be intentional about getting to know people who will build you up.** Hebrews 3:13 (NIV)

37. **Mentoring is ultimately about getting closer to God.** James 4:7-8 (NIV)

38. **We need the input of a mentor to discern the movement of God in our lives.** Proverbs 19:20 (NIV)

39. **Godly Mentors will point you to seek God in all situations.** Matthew 6:33 (NIV)

40. **Mentoring is as simple as doing life together.** Matthew 18:20 (ESV)

41. **With a mentor you can walk on the path to growing your faith and trusting God.** Ephesians 4:15 (NIV)

42. **Sometimes the smallest details of our day, God reveals the greatest depths of His boundless love.** Psalm 37:23 (NLT)

43. **You will not stumble when you are on your knees in prayer.** Matthew 15:25 (NIV)

44. **Mentoring can make the difference between success and significance.** Matthew 10:29-31 (NIV)

45. **A Mentor will help you develop a strong biblical filter around your mind and heart.** Proverbs 4:23 (NIV)

46. **Keep your conversation open and authentic. No one is perfect. Everyone has brokenness.** Psalm 34:18 (NIV)

47. **Your Mentor can help you move toward contentment in every aspect of your life if you are willing to change.** 2 Corinthians 5:17 (NIV)

48. **Yes, life is not easy. But be encouraged...restoration is in the heart of God.** 1 Peter 5:10 (NIV)

49. **A mentoring relationship can help you discover who you are in Christ with fresh eyes and a hopeful heart.** Isaiah 40:31 (NIV)

50. **You don't have to do life alone and in despair. Pursue a mentoring relationship and successfully change the odds.** Genesis 2:18 (NIV)

APPENDIX D: DISCUSSION QUESTIONS TO SUSTAIN YOUR CONVERSATIONS:

- How can I help your relationship with Jesus Christ grow?
- What's happening in your Life Group this month?
- Have you been thinking and praying over the current headlines in the news this week?
- Have you ever considered serving on a mission trip?
- How is your work environment? Do you think your co-workers know you are a Christian?
- If you could change one thing in your life right now what would it be?
- How is your commitment to prayer going this week?
- Do you have a life verse? If you could pick one, what would it be?
- How have you seen the Lord at work in your life this week?
- How are you and God doing today?
- What is holding you back from fully trusting God?
- What do you think God is asking you to do or to learn in this situation?
- What do you like best about your job? Least?
- In what part of your life do you feel most vulnerable?
- Tell me more. What's not working?
- What is keeping you up at night? Why?
- How long has this been a problem? What have you tried so far?
- Have you given up trying to deal with this situation?
- What do you sense God is doing here? How do you know?
- How committed to change in this area are you?
- What are you prepared to do?
- What's God calling you to do?

APPENDIX E: RECOMMENDED RESOURCES TO GROW YOUR FAITH AND CONVERSATIONS

A Praying Life: Connecting With God In A Distracting World
By Paul E. Miller

Becoming A Women of Strength (and other books in this Becoming a Woman of Series)
By Cynthia Heald

Chase The Lion: If Your Dream Doesn't Scare You, It's Too Small
By Mark Batterson

Communicating For A Change
By Andy Stanley and Lane Jones

Experiencing God Around The Kitchen Table
By Marilynn Blackaby and Carrie Blackaby Webb

Experiencing God: Knowing and Doing the Will Of God
By Henry T. Blackaby and Claude V. King

Glory Days: Living Your Promised Land Life Now
By Max Lucado

If God Is Good: Faith in the Midst of Suffering and Evil
By Randy Alcorn

Life In the Balance: Biblical Answers for the Issues of Our Day
By Joni Eareckson Tada and friends

Living Among Lions: How To Thrive Like Daniel In Today's Babylon
By David and Jason Benham

Spiritual Leadership Coaching: Connecting People to God's Heart and Purpose
By Richard Blackaby and Bob Royall

Telling Yourself The Truth: Find Your Way Out of Depression, Anxiety, Fear, Anger, and other Common Problems
By William Backus and Marie Chapian

The Grace and Truth Paradox: Responding with Christlike Balance
By Randy Alcorn

The Power Of Your Words: How God can Bless Your Life through The Words You Speak
By Robert Morris

The Unexpected Journey: Conversations with People Who Turned from other Beliefs to Jesus
By Thom S. Rainer

ACKNOWLEDGMENTS

First and foremost, Jesus. Thank you for your unconditional love and encouragement at the perfect needed time.

John, Jered, Lauren, Jason, Sarah, Joanna and Skylar, my incredible family. And to Gabriela, Piper, Sutton, Max Henry and Harper for filling Gammy's love cup to overflowing. Without all of you I'm toast and empty inside. I love you all!

A special thanks to my daughter and best girlfriend, Joanna Lee Murray, for her constant words of encouragement and nudge to keep going no matter what obstacles I had to face.

To all of my Prayer Warriors and Proof readers: Joanna Lee, Sandy Herrmann, SuAnne Wolff, Brittanny White, Ken Babrick, Lindey Newton, Tim Newton, Morgan Canclini-Mitchell, Amy Williams, Laura Captari, Holley Bailey, Angie Lester, Aly Chase, Cybil Murray, Cory Gatliff, Tricia Moose, Kristen Cimorelli, Jeannie D'Amico, Joy Gartzke, Connie Keller, Margaret Kimbrough, Cheryl Maier, Medora Strickland, Allison Dye, Meredith Wheatley, Lea Ann Owens, Hunter Melton, Mitch Simpson, Brittany Klaus, my Mastermind friends, Amy and Aaron Bryant. A special thanks for the cover design to my sweet friend, Kristen Ingebretson.

And to you, the reader: Thank you for participating in this study and passing it on. May you be brave enough to be vulnerable, strong enough to reach out, and may you meet God in new ways as you connect with Him, your mentor and a small group of fellow believers.

NOTES

1   Austin, Charles. "Obituary; Catherine Marshall, 68, Author." *New York Times*,
    March 19, 1983. http://www.nytimes.com/1983/03/19/obituaries/obituary-
    catherine-marshall-68-author.html

2   *The Free Library*. S.v. Catherine Marshall remembered." Retrieved September 14, 2018
    from https://www.thefreelibrary.com/Catherine+Marshall+remembered.-a04713566

3   Bible Atlas. "Zarephath." Accessed September 14, 2018. http://bibleatlas.org/
    zarephath.htm

4   Butler, Kathryn. "The Gift of Mom Guilt." *Christianity Today*, September 25,
    2017. http://www.christianitytoday.com/women/2017/september/gift-of-mom-
    guilt-lean-in-opt-out-gods-call.html

5   Butler, Kathryn. "The Gift of Mom Guilt." *Christianity Today*, September 25,
    2017. http://www.christianitytoday.com/women/2017/september/gift-of-mom-
    guilt-lean-in-opt-out-gods-call.html

6   Alcorn, Randy. "Guilt, God, and Self-Esteem." *Help For Women Under
    Stress* (1986): 97-112. url: https://www.epm.org/resources/2005/Mar/28/
    guilt-god-and-self-esteem/

7   Alcorn, Randy. "Guilt, God, and Self-Esteem." *Help For Women Under
    Stress* (1986): 97-112. url: https://www.epm.org/resources/2005/Mar/28/
    guilt-god-and-self-esteem/

8   Goff, Bob, and The Barna Group. *Multi-Careering: Find Meaning in Your Next
    Season*. Zondervan, 2013.

9   Goff, Bob, and The Barna Group. *Multi-Careering: Find Meaning in Your Next
    Season*. Zondervan, 2013.

10 I Am Second. "Shawn Johnson." Accessed September 14, 2018. http://www.
    iamsecond.com/seconds/shawn-johnson/

11 Heiser, Christina. "How Olympian Shawn Johnson Is Fighting Back Against
    Body Shaming." *Women's Health Magazine*, July 27, 2016. https://www.
    womenshealthmag.com/life/dove-my-beauty-my-say-campaign

12 Gleeson, Scott. "Former Olympian Shawn Johnson Shares Heartbreaking
    Story of Miscarriage." *USA TODAY Sports*, October 21, 2017.
    https://www.usatoday.com/story/sports/olympics/2017/10/21/

former-olympian-shawn-johnson-shares-heartbreaking-story-having-miscarriage/787551001/

13 Carter, Joe. "9 Things You Should Know About Elisabeth Elliot." *The Gospel Coalition*, June 15, 2015. https://www.thegospelcoalition.org/article/9-things-you-should-know-about-elisabeth-elliot/

14 Morgan, Elisa. *She Did What She Could: Five Words of Jesus That Will Change Your Life.* Tyndale House Publishers, 2007.

15 Moody Radio. "In the Market with Janet Parshall." Accessed September 14, 2018. https://www.moodyradio.org/programs/in-the-market-with-janet-parshall/about

16 Wikipedia. "Janet Parshall." Accessed September 14, 2018. https://en.wikipedia.org/wiki/Janet_Parshall

17 Hart, Ann Henderson. "Finding Hope Beyond the Ruins: An Interview with Lisa Beamer." *Modern Reformation* Vol. 11, No. 5 (September/October 2002): 24-31.

18 Beamer, Lisa. "Let's Roll: Exclusive excerpts from Lisa Beamer's book about Flight 93." *World Magazine*, August 17, 2002. http://www.freerepublic.com/focus/news/730909/posts

19 Beamer, Lisa. *Let's Roll!: Ordinary People, Extraordinary Courage.* Tyndale House Publishers, 2002.

20 Discipleship Library. "Emilie Barnes." Accessed September 14, 2018. http://turret2.discipleshiplibrary.com/8036A.mp3 also, http://www.discipleshiplibrary.com/

21 Tada, Joni Eareckson. "Reflections on the 50th Anniversary of My Driving Accident" *The Gospel Coalition*, July 30, 2017. https://www.thegospelcoalition.org/article/reflections-on-50th-anniversary-of-my-diving-accident/

22 Joni and Friends. "Joni's Bio." Accessed September 14, 2018. https://www.joniandfriends.org/jonis-corner/jonis-bio/

ABOUT THE AUTHOR

Jayme Hull was born in Littlestown, Pennsylvania, and received Christ as her personal Savior at eighteen years old while studying at New York University. In 1980 she married her best friend John, who was her high school sweetheart. She is the mom to three adult married children to three amazing spouses and Gammy to five grandchildren.

Jayme is the author of *Face To Face: Discover How Mentoring Can Change Your Life*, host of the *Face To Face Mentoring Podcast* and writes for her website www.JaymeLeeHull.com

She frequently speaks and shares the mentoring message at events and with any size group interested in making an impact on the next generation. She loves to share the joy of the Lord, be with her husband and family, watch a good musical, and spend time talking over a cup of coffee and hearing others God stories.

CONTINUE THE CONVERSATION
BLOG JaymeLeeHull.com
FACEBOOK JaymeHullFaceToFaceMentoring
TWITTER JaymeHull

***Face To Face: Discover How Mentoring Can Change Your Life* (Moody Publishers)**
Available on Amazon or www.JaymeLeeHull.com

Whether you have a mentor, can't seem to find one, or haven't even thought to look, Jayme Hull walks you through every aspect of this critical relationship. Packed with stories and anecdotes from Jayme's experience as both a mentor and mentee—plus sprinklings of wisdom on balance, purpose, and change—*Face to Face* speaks to the heart of young Christian s eager to grow. In her warm, personable style, Jayme offers expert advice on how to journey well with someone further along.